T0088143

TALES FROM THE
MINNESOTA GOPHERS

A COLLECTION OF THE GREATEST
GOPHER STORIES EVER TOLD

RAY CHRISTENSEN
WITH DAVE MONA

SPORTS
PUBLISHING

Sports Publishing books may be purchased in bulk at special discounts
for sales promotion, corporate gifts, fund-raising, or educational
purposes. Special editions can also be created to specifications. For
details, contact the Special Sales Department, Sports Publishing,
307 West 36th Street, 11th Floor, New York, NY 10018 or
sportspubbooks@skyhorsepublishing.com.

Sports Publishing® is a registered trademark of Skyhorse Publishing,
Inc.®, a Delaware corporation.

Visit our website at www.sportspubbooks.com.

10 9 8 7 6 5 4 3 2 1

Library of Congress Cataloging-in-Publication Data is available on file.

ISBN: 978-1-61321-440-4

Printed in the United States of America

*To my wife, Ramona, and to the
University of Minnesota Men's Athletics
Department, both always supportive in
my fifty years of collecting memories.*

—RC

_____

Editor's Note: The stories before
the epilogue have been left as
originally published in 2002.

Contents

Basketball

Golf

Baseball

Tennis

Swimming

Epilogue

Preface

Gopher football and basketball are the sports most frequently represented in this book, but all of the men's sports at the University of Minnesota are included. This book would not be complete without them.

Most of the events and stories take place in the second hald of the twentieth century, my span of broadcasting years, but at the same time, Bronko Nagurski, the Bierman years and other earlier remembrances are included. These are the fabric of my boyhood dreams, and I hope I have given them their due.

—RC

Acknowledgments

Above all, I thank the University of Minnesota Men's Athletics Department, Marc Ryan, Bill Crumley and the entire Media Relations staff, photographers Wendell Vandersluis, Jerry Lee and Michelle King, and all the coaches and their staffs. Without their knowledge, suggestions and years of documents, without their friendship, this book would not have been possible.

I am grateful to many publications. They helped jog my memory, confirm my memory and, in some cases, refute my memory, steering me in the right direction.
These include:
50 Years, 50 Heroes
The College Football Hall of Fame by Kent Stephens
The Big Ten by Tug Wilson and Jerry Brondfield
Gopher Sketchbook by Al Papas, Jr.
100 Years of Golden Gopher Football, edited by Ralph Turtinen
Pigskin Pride by Ross Bernstein
Gopher Glory, edited by Steve Perlstein
Fifty years of University of Minnesota Men's Athletics media publications

—RC

Football

The Hall of Traditions

As you enter the Gibson-Nagurski Hall of Traditions, the main entrance to the football complex, the towering, revolving, golden statue of Bronko Nagurski looms to your immediate left. Five separate displays line the long wall ahead to your left.

The first is devoted to the Bronk and to George Gibson, his All-American guard, who helped open holes for Nagurski.

The subsequent displays are:

A Tradition of Leadership-coaches through the years.

A Tradition of Talent-players through the years. The jerseys of Bronko Nagurski, Bruce Smith, Paul Giel and Sandy Stephens. The Outland Award trophies of Tom Brown and Bobby Bell, Tyrone Carter's 1999 Jim Thorpe Award trophy for Best Defensive Back. There's a somewhat deflated football from 1909, inscribed Minnesota 20-Chicago 6.

A Tradition of Competition-bowl trophies, rivalry trophies (the actual trophy if Minnesota is in current possession, photo displays if it's not).

A Tradition of Victory-national championship trophies (very handsome) and others. One of these you may not have heard of: the 1961 Bob Zuppke Award to "The Best Football Team with the Most Demanding Schedule."

The displays also include video screens. You touch the screen, and visual and audio Golden Gopher history comes to

Part of the North Wall of the Hall of Traditions

life. The hall is two stories high. The upper half of the left wall features, from left to right, a large photograph of a very early Minnesota football team and large cut-out action figures of Bruce Smith, Sandy Stephens, Bobby Bell, and Tyrone Carter.

Centered at the far end of the hall is a goal post, not full-size, but still impressively large. The base of the support is well-padded, in case you're still looking back over your shoulder at what you've been seeing. The right wall has windows but also two more small display areas.

One hundred-twenty years of University of Minnesota football.

There is room for more names, more trophies, more tradition.

There will be more.

Doc Williams

In the latter part of the 19th century, Henry L. Williams was a good halfback and an even better hurdler (he set a world record) at Yale.

After graduation, he became a high school teacher at a small town not far from West Point. In August of 1891, he took a horse and buggy to West Point to do a little coaching. He did well enough that the Army gridders beat Navy for the first time.

Turning to medicine, Williams got his M.D. in Pennsylvania in 1895. Then in 1900, Amos Alonzo Stagg (a former teammate at Yale) suggested to the University of Minnesota that it hire the doctor as its football coach. Williams accepted Minnesota's bid, with the provision that he be allowed to continue his medical practice. Thus he became the Gophers' first full-time salaried football coach.

In his first season, Williams led the Gophers to an unbeaten record: 9 wins, 2 ties. He went on to coach Minnesota for 22 years, the longest tenure of any Gopher coach (Murray Warmath had 18 seasons, Bernie Bierman, 16). In that span, Doc Williams had eight Big Ten championships and an overall record of 136-33-11. In 1950, the University of Minnesota Fieldhouse was renamed Williams Arena.

Despite that horse and buggy he took to coach at West Point, his was never a horse-and-buggy operation. In 1904, as a member of the rules committee, he proposed legalizing the forward pass. It took two years, but in 1906, the pass became legal.

Williams was the first coach to use a flanker in a passing formation. His seven-man defensive line remained the standard for over two decades.

His most renowned innovation was the Williams Shift. Until 1910, all backfield members took a frozen position until the ball was snapped. Even the advent of the pass did not change the "freeze." Williams created a revolution. The backs took their traditional set position. Then, just before the ball was snapped, they sprang into different positions. The defense had no time to adjust, and the offense gained a huge advantage. It was legal, but nobody had ever done it before Doc Williams. (Many years later, the rules committee decided that all four backs would have to come to a full stop for at least a second before the snap of the ball).

In his twenty-two seasons of championships and innovations, Henry L. Williams never had more than one assistant coach at a time, and the good doctor continued to maintain a thriving medical practice.

John McGovern

John McGovern was one of Minnesota's first All-Americans (1909). Lettering from 1908 to 1910, he quarterbacked the Gophers to Big Ten championships his last two years. An outstanding runner, punter, and drop-kicker on offense, he was equally efficient on defense. Minnesota outscored its opponents 158-27 in 1909 and 179-6 in 1910, gaining ten shutouts in those two 7-game seasons. The Gophers were 6-1 each season, losing twice to Michigan.

McGovern missed only one game in three seasons, playing every minute of all the other games.

John McGovern was five feet, five inches in height. He stands tall in the College Football Hall of Fame.

Bronko

You're just inside the Gibson-Nagurski Football Complex at the University of Minnesota, and there's this huge golden statue of a football player, far more than life-size. A small circular plaque tells you it is Bronko Nagurski, whose legendary career has reached almost mythical proportions.

"Bronko" in the Hall of Traditions

Bronko was born Bronislav, but his mother took pity on his early teachers and suggested Bronko. The name absorbed permanence, to the degree that many of Nagurski's legal documents read Bronko, not Bronislav.

One of the Bronko myths is that Minnesota's head football coach, Clarence "Doc" Spears, recruiting near International Falls, came upon a young man, operating a hand plow behind two horses. Spears asked directions. The young man did not raise his arm to point the way. He raised the plow.*

Actually, Nagurski always wanted to play for Minnesota and came to the school on his own.

As a freshman (not eligible in those days), he demoralized the varsity during the week as a fullback on offense and tackle and end on defense. In 1927-28-29, he became, according to sportswriter Grantland Rice, "possibly the greatest football player of all time."

The Gophers never won a Big Ten title in Nagurski's three years, finishing 18-4-2. Of the four losses, three were by one point, the fourth by two.

In 1929, Bronko Nagurski was listed as an All-American at fullback on offense and at tackle on defense. Another All-America first team had him at defensive end. It is said that the Bronk, at one time or another, played every position but quarterback.

After his Gopher career, Nagurski went on to play fullback and linebacker for the Chicago Bears. He rushed for 4,031 yards in his eight seasons, a huge number in those years of much shorter schedules.

Bears owner George Halas reluctantly paid him $5,000 the first year, then cut his salary the second season. Nagurski finally got back up to the $5,000 mark in 1937.

Bronko retired then, but with the wartime manpower crunch in 1943, he was persuaded to come back for one more year. Playing tackle only, he helped the Bears win another title.

Bronko Nagurski died in 1990 at his home in International Falls, Minnesota. In 1992, the Bronko Nagurski Museum opened in Smokey Bear Park in the Falls. In 1995, the Football Writers Association of America voted to attach his name to one of college football's most prestigious annual awards: The Nagurski Defensive Player of the Year.

Take another look at that revolving statue as you leave the Gibson-Nagurski Football Complex.

It's the right size.

* The "pointing with the plow" story was repeated later with coach Bernie Bierman, but Doc Spears and Nagurski were first.

Bernie's Golden Decade

Unquestionably, the most "golden" years of Golden Gopher football were the ten years from 1932 to 1941. In 1932, Bernie Bierman was named head coach at his alma mater. In his first year, Minnesota won 5 and lost 3. Not bad, but the second year became the real indicator of what lay ahead. The Gophers won 4 and tied 4 (2 wins, 4 ties in Big Ten games).

In 1934 and 35, Minnesota won all 8 games. In 1936, a 6-0 loss to Northwestern ended a string of 21 straight victories (29 straight games without a loss). However, the team still went 7 and 1 that season. The University of Minnesota won the national championship all three of those years, and Bernie Bierman is still the only major college coach ever to win three consecutive crowns.

Additional national titles came in 1940 and 1941.*

In 1942, Bierman was called into military service (his Iowa Seahawks team defeated the Gophers twice, both close games). When he returned in 1945, college football was changing. The single wing, which Bierman teams executed to near-perfection, was fading in popularity, while more and more coaches turned to the T-formation. Bierman postwar teams still went 29-16 until 1950. By then, most of the returning servicemen had used up their eligibility. The 1950 Gophers went 1-7-1, and Bierman's 16th season at the University was his last.

What of those golden years, though? From 1932 through 1941, Minnesota was the Big Ten champion seven times, national champion five times. In that decade, the Gophers compiled a 63-12-5 record. Bierman coached thirteen All-Americans and in 1955 was inducted into the College Football Hall of Fame.

No coach ever deserved it more.

* See "The Return to the Top"

Kostka and the Draft

Stan Kostka's first year at Minnesota was 1934. That national championship team had such great depth that Kostka was the backup fullback. In 1935, however, Kostka not only started but earned All-American honors. He led the Big Ten in scoring and was seventh in the nation in that category.

The next year, his senior year, never materialized.

Kostka played as a freshman at Oregon in the Pacific Coast Conference before transferring to Minnesota. The Big Ten did not permit freshmen to play, so after Kostka's sophomore and junior years, the conference ruled that with three years of competition, he had used up his eligibility. Learning this, pro teams began a bidding war for Kostka. The result: a $5,000 contract, with a $500 bonus, big money in the mid-thirties.

That bidding war posed such unpleasant consequences that professional football instituted the college draft in 1936.

Gophers... Golden Gophers

In 1857, a published cartoon showed nine Gopher bodies with the heads of local politicians, pulling a locomotive. The accompanying story covered a bill in the state legislature proposing five million dollars for railroad expansion in western Minnesota. Somehow, that cartoon triggered the imagination of many residents of the territory, and they started calling themselves "Gophers," some in jest, some seriously. The University of Minnesota took it seriously enough to choose "Gophers" as its nickname.

"Golden Gophers" was coined in the 1930s by sports writer/broadcaster Halsey Hall when Bernie Bierman's Gophers changed to all-gold uniforms. They were a dull gold and not particularly attractive, but that only made the powerhouse teams of the thirties seem all the more intimidating.

The Return to the Top

In 1939, Bernie Bierman had his first losing season as Minnesota's head coach (3-4-1). The Gophers not only rebounded the very next year, they regained the national championship they had held in 1934-35-36. It wasn't easy. Minnesota went 8 and 0, but five of the eight wins were by six points or less. In the season opener, Sonny Franck's 98-yard kickoff return made the difference in a 19-14 win over Washington. In game two, Bruce Smith hit Bill Daley on a 42-yard scoring pass in a 13-7 victory. Game three was also a 13-7 triumph, with Franck tackling an Ohio State runner on the one-yard line as the game ended. An easy win over Iowa was followed by a 13-12 squeaker over Northwestern and a 7-6 decision over Michigan. In that game, Bruce Smith ran 80 yards on a reverse for the only Gopher score, and from Minnesota's 3-yard line, at the end of the game, Tom Harmon failed to score on three plunges. (Harmon never did score against Minnesota in his illustrious career). The final two games were easier, victories over Purdue and Wisconsin.

Incidentally, Minnesota threw only three passes in the wins over Nebraska, Ohio State and Iowa, on successive Saturdays. All three went for touchdowns.

The Talking Play

Minnesota won the national crown again in 1941, going 8 and 0 again, and this time only two games were nail-biters. They came back to back. The Gophers beat Michigan, 7-0, when Bruce Smith hit Herm Frickey on a 43-yard pass that set up Frickey's touchdown run. Shortly after that, Smith suffered a leg injury that took him out for the rest of the game.

The next week, Minnesota faced Northwestern. The year before, the Gophers had escaped with a 13-12 win, and Bernie Bierman felt this year's game could be just as close. Before the game, he warned the officials that Minnesota might use the "Talking Play." It turned out the play was indeed necessary.

Bruce Smith started this game, but his leg injury sidelined him. The Gophers had scored on a bad-snap safety, but the Wildcats countered on a touchdown pass from Otto Graham to Bud Hasse. It was 7-2 Northwestern, and without Smith, Minnesota's offense was sputtering. Then Ed Lechner blocked a Wildcat punt, and the Gophers had the ball. From the bench, Bierman signaled for the "Talking Play." Minnesota ran the ball for one yard, going out of bounds, forcing the officials to bring the ball in for the next play. Center Gene Flick stood by the ball, while all the other linemen stood casually at the line of scrimmage, to Flick's right. The backs were also casually in place, everyone motionless. Flick quickly grabbed the ball and flipped it to scatback Bud Higgins. Helped by the element of surprise and by two solid blocks thrown by Urban Odson, Higgins scampered for the winning score. 8-7 Minnesota, and the Gophers went on to their second straight national championship.

Franck, Smith and the Heisman

When Minnesota won the national championship in 1940, the offense was led by George "Sonny" Franck and Bruce Smith.

Some football analysts felt Franck would have won the Heisman Trophy that year had he not been paired with Smith. Both were so gifted, offensively and defensively, that they undoubtedly took votes from each other. As it was, Franck and tackle Urban Odson were named All-Americans in 1940. Franck was third runner-up for the Heisman.*

In 1941, Franck had graduated, the Gophers repeated as national champs, and Bruce Smith was not only named as an All-American** but became Minnesota's only winner of the Heisman, college football's highest honor.

The Faribault, Minnesota native's 1941 statistics are not overwhelming, but he was a winner. When Minnesota was behind in a game, Smith's pass or run put them ahead to stay. Against Nebraska, Ohio State and Iowa, he completed just one pass in each game. All three of those passes were for touchdowns. Against Iowa, after one quarter, Minnesota had zero yards rushing. The injured Smith persuaded coach Bierman to let him play. That turned the game around, and Minnesota won it, 34-13.

As a runner, passer, blocker, tackler and, above all, leader, team captain Smith was everything the Heisman Trophy symbolizes.

Bruce Smith died of cancer August 26th, 1967, at the age of forty-seven. In the months preceding his death, he worked tirelessly, visiting and bringing hope to young cancer patients.

In 1972, Smith was named to the College Football Hall of Fame. In 1977, his number, 54, became the first Minnesota numeral to be retired.

* Franck was also a three-time letter winner in track and field.

* * Tackle Dick Wildung was also named All-American in 1941 and repeated in 1942.

The Drop-Kick

In 1934, the shape of the football was changed. The end tips of the ball, which had a rounded, snub-nosed appearance, now became pointed. The change made a bouncing ball far less predictable and improved the "spiral" capability. It also started the drop-kick on its way out. With the drop-kick, the field goal or extra point kicker got a direct snap (no holder), dropped the ball, then kicked it just as it came back off the turf. It was not as effective as today's snap-place-kick, but it was far more entertaining.

The last recorded Gopher drop-kick came in the 1942 game against Michigan. With time running out in the first half and no time for a snap-and-hold alignment, Bill Garnaas took the snap from center and drop-kicked a field goal that proved to be the winning margin in a 16-14 Minnesota win.

Memorial Stadium, the Inside Story

Memorial Stadium was dedicated in 1924 to the memory of Minnesotans who died in World War I. The football field was encircled by a running track. In 1948, the University of Minnesota won the national track and field championship in Memorial Stadium. I broadcast several live segments of the event on KUOM, the University radio station. That was my first play-by-play and the only time I covered track and field.

On November 18, 1961, the largest-ever crowd for a football game watched the Gophers defeat Purdue, 10-7. That Minnesota team went on to win the Rose Bowl. The attendance, depending on the source, was either 66,284 or 67,081. Either one was well above the official capacity of 63,555. A remodeling in 1970 reduced the capacity to 56,652.

The "inside story" of Memorial Stadium is something far more important than any sporting event ever held there. Starting in 1940, if you entered the stadium at Gate 27, you'd find the

Memorial Stadium and (top) Williams Arena in the 1970s

Laboratory of Physiological Hygiene headed by Dr. Ancel Keys. Using conscientious objectors (to World War II) and other volunteers, Dr. Keys conducted a study on starvation that is still a worldwide research reference. His study in nutrition quickly helped develop the K-ration, very familiar to the military in the war. Keys' continuing research had and still has a major impact on the fields of medicine and science, stressing such areas as nutrition, cholesterol, exercise, lifestyles and infinitely more. Dr. Ancel Keys' research institution is now part of the University's School of Public Health and Division of Epidemiology.

As a football home, Memorial Stadium had its fifty-eighth and final season in 1981. When the stadium was taken down, many of its one million bricks were made available for sale to the public. I have one of them.

The main arch of Memorial Stadium was dismantled, brick by brick (over 7,000 bricks), stone by stone (92 pieces of stone), and now forms an imposing, tilted (15 degrees off vertical), fifty-foot tall, seventy-ton entrance to the Carlson Heritage Gallery in the McNamara Center (see "Pinky"). The arch is located about a football field's distance from where it once stood.

The Rouser

In 1909, the *Minneapolis Tribune* sponsored a contest to find a fight song for University of Minnesota athletics, the winner getting one hundred dollars. The judges were the governor of Minnesota, A. O. Eberhardt, and university president Cyrus Northrop. Floyd M. Hutsell's composition won the hundred, a pretty fair sum in 1909.

"Rah-rah-rah for Ski-U-Mah" is part of the Rouser, and that phrase dates back to 1884. Minnesota had a rugby team then, and two of its players, Win Sargent and John Adams, decided the team needed a victory cheer. Some research uncovered "Ski-oo," a Sioux battle cry of victory. Sargent and Adams added "Mah," because it rhymed with "Rah-rah-rah." The "oo" became "U" for University, and the "M" in "Mah" apparently represented Minnesota.

"Rah-rah-rah for Ski-U-Mah" has become an integral part of virtually every Gopher sporting event.

Let's Hear It for the Gophers!

Ski-U-Mah dates back to 1884. College cheerleading began fourteen years later, and it started at the University of Minnesota. Johnny Campbell first led organized cheers at the Minnesota-Northwestern football game of November 12, 1898. The Gophers, coming off three straight losses, beat the Wildcats. Cheerleading was here to stay at Minnesota, and, gradually, it spread nationwide.

Campbell was truly a loyal Gopher fan. He never missed a home game for over forty years.

The most active early cheerleader was Russell Rathbun, the Big Ten champion in the one-mile run. Nicknamed "Bunny" because he did all kinds of gymnastics to get the crowd involved, the 5-foot-5-inch Rathbun also originated the use of an all-white uniform.

College football's first female cheerleaders debuted at Marquette in 1927, but women did not enter the cheerleading scene at Minnesota until World War II and then only because of the manpower shortage. They proved themselves immediately and have been an integral part of Golden Gopher spirit support ever since.

Bud

He came to the University of Minnesota from Superior, Wisconsin, and he came on his own. No scholarship. Also, no pressure to limit him to one sport.

Harry "Bud" Grant, as versatile an athlete as any who ever played at Minnesota, earned nine letters in three sports from 1947 to 1949, excelling in all three sports. Twice an All-Big Ten end in football, he started at forward all three seasons in basketball, and in baseball, he was a leading hitter and gifted outfielder for three years.

Bud also listened, observed and took what worked for him from his Gopher coaches: Bernie Bierman in football, Dave MacMillan and Ozzie Cowles in basketball, and Dick Siebert in baseball (MacMillan was also the baseball coach in 1947).

After two seasons with the Minneapolis Lakers, Grant switched to football. Two seasons with the Philadelphia Eagles were followed by four years as a player, then ten more as head coach, for the Winnipeg Blue Bombers. From there, he came south to the Minnesota Vikings, where his eighteen seasons as head coach led to his enshrinement in the Pro Football Hall of Fame in 1994.*

Bud Grant's University of Minnesota career ended in 1949. My Gopher play-by-play career began in 1951, but I was fortunate enough to call the Vikings games in the late sixties. There I got to know Bud Grant, as a coach and as a friend. In both capacities, he is the best anyone could want.

*Three other Gophers preceded Bud into Canton, Ohio: charter member Bronko Nagurski in 1963, Leo Nomellini (Grant's teammate at the University) in 1969, and Bobby Bell in 1983.

The $2.50 Limit

In the early summer of 1951, I learned that the University of Minnesota Athletics Department needed someone to do the play-by-play of Gopher football games on KUOM, the university radio station.

I was the chief announcer at KUOM (actually, the only full-time announcer). The play-by-play job would not enlarge my salary. The network for these noncommercial broadcasts had dwindled to four stations, so no fee was available. However, the challenge and the opportunity were what was important to me, so I had our program director, Bun Dawson, submit my name. I had been doing the public address work for the University Marching Band's halftime shows, so the Athletics Department was familiar with my voice, and Bun enlarged my qualifications to the stretching point.

The summer came and went with no word, no audition and no interview, but also with no announcement of anyone being named to the job. The first game was scheduled for Saturday, September 29, against Washington. I prepared for it as if I had already been chosen. Monday morning, September 24, I called Athletics Director Ike Armstrong's office. His secretary answered. I identified myself and asked whether a play-by-play decision had been made.

"Oh, yes," she replied. "I've been meaning to call you. When you're doing an away game, you can't charge more than $2.50 a meal on your expense report."

50 years, 510 Gopher football games and 2 more radio stations later, I retired.

The Single Wing Surprise

My first year of Gopher football broadcasting, 1951, was Wes Fesler's first year as head coach. The trend away from the single wing to the T-formation was well underway, and Fesler was a part of it.

Minnesota dropped its first three games, a tough 25-20 loss to Washington, an embarrassing 55-14 drubbing at California, and a 21-7 defeat at the hands of Northwestern.

Next came Homecoming against favored Nebraska. Fesler decided to return to the single wing, but naturally did not reveal his decision publicly. Paul Giel was moved from quarterback to left halfback.

The change caught the Cornhuskers off guard. Giel totaled well over 200 yards, running and passing, and the Gophers knocked off Nebraska, 39-20.

In the next game, the single wing was effective but no longer a surprise, and Michigan outscored Minnesota 54-27.

The Best Runs

In a separate story, I cover Rickey Foggie's 31-yard scramble that set up Chip Lohmiller's winning field goal against Michigan at Ann Arbor in 1986. Other thrilling runs: Darrell Thompson's 98-yard run, also against Michigan, a year later. Darrell went down the right sideline past the Michigan bench. The Wolverines won that game, though, 30-20. Bob McNamara's 89-yard kickoff return against Iowa in 1954 made the difference in a 22-20 Gopher win. McNamara had 209 yards in total offense in the first half alone.

My all-time favorite came in 1951, my first year and Paul
Giel's first year. In the second quarter, with Purdue leading 19-0,
Giel dropped back to pass, found no one open, and began to run.
Even getting back to the line of scrimmage was a struggle. Thereafter, several Boilermakers had a second try at tackling him (Paul
always says of himself, "I wasn't big, but I was slow."). After what
seemed an eternity, he broke clear for an incredible 64-yard touchdown. Minnesota scored again before the half to make it 19-13,
but the second half was remarkably scoreless, and Purdue won the
game.

Paul Giel's greatest game was against Michigan in 1953,
the fiftieth anniversary of the Little Brown Jug. Paul ran the ball 35
times for 112 yards, completed 13 of 18 passes for 169 yards and a
touchdown, returned a kickoff 24 yards, averaged 59 yards a punt
on 4 punts and, on defense, intercepted 2 passes. Minnesota 22 -
Michigan 0.*

* A Giel all-purpose predecessor was Harold Van Every. In 1937,
he led the Gophers in running, passing, kickoff and punt returns,
punting and interceptions. He was named to *Sports Illustrated*'s
Silver Anniversary All-American Team.

Unswerving Loyalty

On November 24, 1951, my first year of play-by-play, Minnesota and Wisconsin played their season closer at Memorial Stadium. The temperature was not too far from zero. The wind chill
reading had a minus sign on it.

Obviously, I did not hear the following exchange, but I got
the story from more than one source. It was late in the game. The
Gophers were losing 30-6 and were about to finish with a 2-6-1
record. In the press box (the only room with heat), Minnesota
Athletics Director Ike Armstrong and a member of the Wisconsin
administrative staff stood next to each other.

The Badger supporter turned to Armstrong and said admiringly, "I've got to hand it to your fans, Ike. Most of them are still here. That's loyalty for you."

Armstrong, for whom any form of profanity was unusual, replied: "Loyalty, hell. They're frozen in place."

The "1" and "2" Return

Dick "Pinky" McNamara and his older brother Bob played on the same Gopher team for just one season, 1954. They were the two deep men on kickoff returns.

Coach Murray Warmath added a play in which one brother would hand the ball off to the other on a kick return reverse. If the play called was "1," Bob would hand off to Pinky, if a "2," Pinky delivered the ball to Bob. The play was successful more than once, but it was always a "2," Bob getting the handoff.

Pinky approached Coach Warmath during the week and wondered if the "1" return would ever be called.

Warmath replied, "Maybe next year, when your brother has graduated."

Minnesota and Iowa - the Biggest Game

The Minnesota-Iowa football rivalry was once a bitter one (see "The Jug and the Hog"). By the time I began covering the Gophers in 1951, it was still an intense rivalry but fortunately less bitter.

In my fifty years, I called fifty games between the Gophers and the Hawkeyes. Minnesota won 25, Iowa 23, and two ended in ties.

The most heralded game in those fifty meetings came on November 5, 1960. I had described nine Minnesota-Iowa games at that point, and the U of M record was just 2-6-1. In 1959, at Iowa City, the Hawks had humiliated the Gophers, 33-0.

Both teams came into the 1960 game with 6-0 records. Iowa was ranked first nationally, Minnesota second. The game had been a sellout since early in the season. Many Iowa fans, who did not have tickets, streamed northward anyhow, hoping to find a ticket at almost any price. Hotel rooms were also unavailable at any price.

Minnesota got its first score because of lineman Tom Brown. Murray Warmath said of Brown, "He scared more people on a football field than any other player in Minnesota history." In the first half, Iowa prepared to punt on a fourth down on its own 46-yard line. Brown, lining up opposite the Hawkeye center, scared him enough that his snap sailed back to the Iowa 14. Three plays later, Bill Munsey scored on a pitchout from Sandy Stephens.

In the third quarter, with the game tied 7-7, Iowa was third and goal on the Minnesota 5-yard line. Brown drove an Iowa guard into quarterback Wilburn Hollis, decking him, for a five-yard loss. The Hawkeyes had to settle for a field goal. 10-7 Iowa, but from there on in, it was all Minnesota.

Sandy Stephens, who played both ways like most players in 1960, was given a breather, and backup quarterback Joe Salem led a Gopher march that featured a 28-yard pass to fullback Roger Hagberg. Stephens came back in to score on a quarterback sneak for the go-ahead touchdown.

In the fourth quarter, Minnesota scored twice more, on a 42-yard run by Hagberg and another quarterback sneak, this time by Salem.

The final: 27-10 Minnesota.

The following week, Purdue upset the maroon and gold, 23-14.

The Gophers ended the season 8-1. Iowa and Minnesota tied for the Big Ten title with 6-1 records, but the win on November 5 put the Gophers into their first Rose Bowl.

The 1962 Rose Bowl

Minnesota has not played in many bowl games, but the unquestioned biggest Gopher bowl victory came January 1, 1962, in the Rose Bowl.

A year earlier, in Minnesota's only other Rose Bowl appearance, the team played a tentative first half. Washington built a 17-0 lead and then withstood a second-half Gopher comeback to win, 17-7.

In '62, the opponent was UCLA. The Bruins kicked a field goal midway through the first quarter, and that ended their scoring. Minnesota got the next 21 to win, 21-3. The Gopher defense was stifling. UCLA totaled just 55 yards rushing, 52 passing.

A year earlier, against Washington, quarterback Sandy Stephens was 2 for 10 passing, with 3 interceptions. This time, he connected on 7 of 11 for 75 yards and ran for 46 yards, including 2 touchdowns.

I did not begin broadcasting for WCCO (the CBS station and thus the Rose Bowl station) until July of 1963, but I did do the play-by-play of all the other Sandy Stephens Gopher games. I will always remember his love for the game and his unquenchable spirit.

Father Knows Best

One of Bobby Bell's fondest memories of his Gopher years is when his father made the trip from Shelby, North Carolina, to see his son play in Memorial Stadium.

In that game, Bell was sidelined in the first half with three cracked ribs. In the locker room, Bell was lying on his back on the training table, getting taped up, when he saw his father standing in the doorway.

Mr. Bell asked trainer Lloyd Stein if Bobby could play without aggravating the injury. Stein said he could. Bobby's father walked over to his son, looked down at him and said, "I didn't come all the way out here to watch you lying on a table. Get out there and play."

Bell, playing with pain, responded with one of the best halves of his career.

The Worst Call

The 1962 Gopher football team, led by Bobby Bell, thrived on defense. It started the season with a scoreless tie with Missouri. It shut out Navy (the Midshipmen lost 31 yards on the ground). In the Big Ten, it blanked Michigan 17-0 (minus 46 yards rushing for the Wolverines), Illinois 17-0 and Iowa 10-0.

Going into the final game at Wisconsin, Minnesota had only one loss, 34-22 to Northwestern. In the other seven games, opponents scored a total of 13 points.

The Gophers led the Badgers 9-7 in the fourth quarter. Badger quarterback Ron VanderKelen dropped back to pass. Bobby Bell charged through, hit VanderKelen and jarred the ball loose, into the hands of Minnesota's Jack Perkovich. Film of the game showed the quarterback still had the ball when Bell made his hit, but an official called a 15-yard penalty on Bell for roughing the passer. An irate Murray Warmath charged the official and drew another 15 yards. Instead of the Gophers having the ball at midfield, Wisconsin had it on the Minnesota 13. The Badgers went in to score and won the game, 14-9.

The week after the Gopher season ended, Bobby Bell was honored at halftime of the Army-Navy game. President John F. Kennedy shook Bell's hand and said, "I thought you really got robbed in the Wisconsin game."

The Outland Award - Brown and Bell - Back to Back

Two University of Minnesota football players have won the Outland Award, given to the best interior lineman in the nation, and they did it in successive years.

In 1961, Tom Brown came in second for the Heisman Trophy, almost unheard-of for a lineman. He won the Outland, was All-American, All Big Ten and the Most Valuable Player in the Big Ten.

A dominating force offensively and defensively, Brown would clear the way for Gopher running backs on offense. On defense, he is best remembered for the way he would drive opposing blockers into the ball carrier, knocking that carrier down without actually touching him. His coach, Murray Warmath, called Brown "a one-man interior line."

Brown never played in the National Football League, but he had many outstanding years with the British Columbia Lions in the Canadian Football League.

In 1962, another Minnesota lineman, tackle Bobby Bell, won the Outland Award. Where Brown came to Minnesota from Minneapolis Central High School, Bell arrived from Shelby, North Carolina, where he had been a high school quarterback. Coach Warmath placed him at tackle, and he made the switch with gusto. At 6 feet 4 inches and with an incredible wing span plus big hands, he often made opposing double-teaming efforts futile with his quick moves and sure tackles.

Bell was named All-American in 1961, then the Outland and unanimous All-American in 1962.* He went on to play NFL football as an All-Pro with the Kansas City Chiefs.

Bobby Bell is enshrined in the College Football Hall of Fame. For no reason that I can come up with, Tom Brown has not yet joined Bell in the Hall.

* Another Gopher, Carl Eller, was runner-up for the Outland in 1963.

Tom Brown-the Outland Award, 1961

Bobby Bell-The Outland Award, 1962

The Helmet Stayed On

Aaron Brown was one of the last two-way players at Minnesota. He played for Murray Warmath in 1963, '64 and '65. Although he is best remembered as a brilliant defensive end, he was also an outstanding end on offense, a solid blocker and a good-hands receiver. He caught 27 passes in 1964, at that time a team record.

Brown's senior year, 1965, was the start of an expanded ten-game schedule for Big Ten schools. This made possible two pre-conference games with Pacific Conference schools. After opening the season with a 20-20 tie with Southern California, the Gophers lost to Washington State, 14-13, a game in which Minnesota gave up the ball on fumbles seven times. Minnesota led 7-0 at the half. In the locker room during halftime, coach Warmath noticed that Brown kept his helmet on. Although that was unusual, Warmath did not question it.

After the game, it turned out that Brown had broken his jaw early in the first quarter. Keeping his helmet on during halftime kept the injury from being noticed.

Aaron Brown played the entire second half, and with his jaw wired shut, went on to earn All-American honors that season.

"We Want Johnson"

I have heard this story several times, but I heard it first and earliest with Murray Warmath as the coach.

Gopher player Johnson put in his practice hours faithfully every weekday, but, come Saturday, he sat on the bench for the entire game. Johnson decided to take matters into his own hands. He enlisted some of his student friends who attended the games to start a chant for him if he didn't get into the game by the second half of the next home game. That game and that second half ar-

rived, and Johnson was in his usual spot- on the bench. He signaled his friends, several rows up in Memorial Stadium.

"We want Johnson... We want Johnson..." No reaction
from Coach Warmath.

Johnson managed to work his way over to the coach's side.

"Ah, coach... they're calling for me."

Coach Warmath looked at him, then stopped to listen.

"We want Johnson... We want Johnson."

"So they are, Johnson. Better get up there and see what
they want."

Murray's Final Game

1971 was Murray Warmath's 18th season as head football
coach at the University of Minnesota. Going into the final game of
the season, a home game against Wisconsin, the Gophers were 3-7
overall, 2-5 in the Big Ten, and had lost four in a row, all conference games. There was considerable speculation that this was
Warmath's final game. The team was well aware of the rumors and
wanted to bring its coach an upset victory in what might well be
the end of his career.

Minnesota played well but trailed the Badgers 21-17 with
two minutes remaining. Starting from his own 20-yard line, quarterback Craig Curry led the way in a drive that netted a maximum
of yardage in a minimum of time. In the game's final seconds,
Curry hit Mel Anderson with a 12-yard scoring pass,* and the Gophers had given one of their finest coaches a 23-21 win in what did
indeed prove to be his final game.

In his eighteen seasons, Murray Warmath had an 87-78-7
record, a national championship, two Big Ten titles, two Rose Bowl
appearances and Minnesota's only Rose Bowl championship.

---

* The pass was Curry's ninth touchdown throw of the season, at the
time a team record.

Murray's Soft Side

As Gopher head football coach for eighteen years, Murray Warmath was always tough but fair. As my broadcast partner after his coaching years, he was completely prepared and always personable.

It was during these years of broadcast partnership that I received a 1977 letter from an educator and Gopher fan in Portage, Wisconsin. He wrote:

"In high school, I was sports editor at Alexander Ramsey (a Twin Cities area high school). After the Rose Bowl loss to Washington, a St. Paul sports columnist wrote a nasty column about Warmath. I was so mad, I wrote to the columnist and chewed him out. A week later, someone called me, impersonating Warmath, and told me I would be invited to the Spring Football Banquet as his guest, because of my letter. He would mail me a ticket.

"Weeks went by and no ticket. So I wrote to Murray, asking if he'd forgotten his invitation. A few nights later, the real Warmath called me and apologized for the prank someone had played. He said there was no banquet but that I could visit a session of spring practice some day of my choice.

"I did. Dick Larson (former Gopher player and then the backfield coach) was at the gate to welcome me. After practice, Warmath said he'd mail me a free pass to the game— which he did. You don't think this kid was a mile high? Wow!

"A year later, in my column in the Ramsey paper, I predicted the Gophers would beat UCLA, 21-3, in the Rose Bowl— and they did!"

Cal's First Win

Similar to Wes Fesler's slow start in 1951, Cal Stoll's first year as head coach, 1972, began with a series of losses, five in all, including drubbings by Colorado and Nebraska. The fifth loss, 28-3 to Purdue, brought a strategy change. Like Fesler's strategy surprise twenty-one years earlier, this was implemented for a homecoming game.

Against Iowa, Stoll went to a no-huddle offense. With quarterback Bob Morgan calling out the plays at the line of scrimmage, the Gopher offense moved almost at will, almost entirely on the ground. With over 400 yards rushing, Minnesota trounced the Hawkeyes, 43-14.

The Gophers won four of their last six games, turning an 0-5 start into a 4-7 season.

Never on Saturday

In 1973, Gil Fash was nearing the end of a Sunday-through-Friday career with the Gophers. Fash had worked hard for almost four years as the quarterback for the scout team, preparing Cal Stoll's offense for its opponent the coming Saturday. Fash had never taken a snap in a regular season game.

The Gophers were 5-4 going into a game at Illinois, the next-to-last game of the season.

Minnesota's first string quarterback, John Lawing, was already out with an injury. At the start of the week, second string quarterback Tony Dungy developed a painful swelling in his throwing arm. Suddenly, Gil Fash was going to start, and someone else ran the scout team.

Illinois became a huge favorite. The game's final statistics seemed to bear that out.

First downs: Illinois 20 - Minnesota 5.

Fash threw 12 passes: 4 were intercepted and only 2 were completed.

But the Gophers had no penalties and no fumbles. The Illini fumbled the ball away 6 times.

Late in the game, one of those fumbles gave Minnesota the ball deep in Illinois territory. Here, Gil Fash had one of his two completions. On a perfect bootleg, Fash kept the ball while the Illini defense smothered the phantom ball carrier. Gil lobbed a pass to tight end Dale Henricksen. He ran untouched into the end zone. Minnesota took the lead, 19-16, and that became the final score.

Incidentally, both Fash and Henricksen were from the state of Illinois.

Movie Buff

Tony Dungy was a Gopher quarterback from 1973 to 1976. He also lettered in basketball in 1974, his only season with the cagers, although he was on hand as an enthusiastic spectator at most home basketball games.

Dungy is on the Minnesota Top Ten career list for touchdown passes, completions, passing yards and total offense. He was twice named Academic All-Big Ten.

What I remember most about the Dungy years are not the football seasons but the basketball seasons. At least once a week, I'd be in the athletics building for a basketball media session. I made a habit of checking the film room. More often than not, there was Tony, watching the film of a Gopher football game from the season just ended, a game against an opponent scheduled again in the season to come. Tony Dungy wanted to be ready. I was certain then that he would become a coach, a very good coach.

After graduating, Dungy played for two years with the Pittsburgh Steelers, then began his coaching career. A year as a part-time assistant for the Gophers was followed by fifteen years as an assistant coach at Pittsburgh, Kansas City and the Minnesota Vikings. At age twenty-five, he was the youngest assistant coach in the National Football League. At age twenty-eight, he was the youngest coordinator in the league. Following four years as the Vikings defensive coordinator, he became the head coach of the Tampa Bay Buccaneers.

Tony Dungy continues to earn the highest regard in the NFL.

He still watches a lot of game films.

A Matter of Inches

So many games, in all sports, are decided by one play, where an inch or two makes a difference in the outcome.

On October 22, 1977, Minnesota played Michigan, the number-one team in the nation, at Memorial Stadium. The Gophers, primed for an upset, completely dominated the first half and led 13-0 with just a handful of seconds left in the half.

Michigan quarterback Rick Leach threw a long pass that went off the hands of his receiver at the two-yard line. An inch or two difference likely would have meant a completion, a touchdown and a lead of just 13-7 at the half.

I felt that the near miss deflated the Wolverines. They never came that close to scoring again, Minnesota got its upset, and Michigan's string of 112 games without being shut out came to an end.

Minnesota 16-Michigan 0.

The Jug and the Hog

Minnesota's Trophy games include Floyd of Rosedale, a bronze pig, for Minnesota vs. Iowa, Paul Bunyan's Axe, a 6-foot trophy, for Minnesota vs. Wisconsin and the Governor's Victory Bell, begun in 1993, for Minnesota vs. Penn State.

However, the most famous trophy in the Big Ten and probably in the nation is the Little Brown Jug.

It began in 1903 when Michigan came to Minneapolis with a 28-game winning streak. The Wolverines left with a 6-6 tie and, unintentionally, without their water jug.

When Michigan coach Fielding Yost wrote, requesting the return of the crockery, L. J. Cooke, Minnesota's Athletics Department head, wrote back, "If you want it, you will have to win it."

The five-gallon jug is filled with scores on the outside. Inside? Well, Dr. Cooke once wrote, "I sometimes think that the jug has been filled with spirits, not alcoholic, but the disembodied spirits of the countless players who have fought for it on the gridiron."

Floyd of Rosedale goes back to 1935. Bitter feelings had surfaced between Minnesota and Iowa football supporters. To help stabilize a potentially volatile situation, Minnesota Governor Floyd B. Olson proposed a wager to Iowa Governor Clyde Herring: A Minnesota prize hog against an Iowa prize hog.

Minnesota (5-0) defeated Iowa (4-0-1), 13-6. Governor Herring personally delivered the Iowa prize hog to Governor Olson. The hog, a donation from Rosedale Farms of Fort Dodge, Iowa, was named Floyd (after the winning governor) of Rosedale.

The original Floyd was replaced by a bronze Floyd of Rosedale, created by Saint Paul, Minnesota sculptor Charles Brioschi.

The Little Brown Jug

Floyd of Rosedale

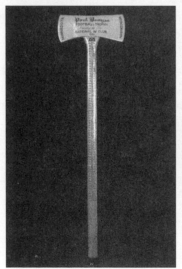

Paul Bunyan's Axe

The Governor's Victory Bell

The Four Football Trophies

Give It to Kent

In 1977, the same year Minnesota shut out Michigan, sophomore back Kent Kitzmann of Rochester, Minnesota set a national record by carrying the ball 57 times in a 21-0 win over Illinois at Champaign. Kitzmann gained 266 yards on those 57 carries. At one point he got 13 consecutive snaps. Illinois' defense knew exactly what was coming, but so strong was Kitzmann and the offensive line ahead of him that not once in those 57 rushes did he lose yardage. That statistic still amazes me.

The following Saturday, in the final game of the regular season, a 13-7 win over Wisconsin, Kitzmann carried the ball only 40 times for 154 yards. The 97 carries in two consecutive games also set a national mark.

Fourth and Ninety-nine

Cal Stoll was head coach of Golden Gopher football for seven years, from 1972 through 1978. I knew him as a coach, as a broadcast partner for Gopher football and, always, as a friend. In all those roles, he was a professional, a gentleman and everlastingly an optimist.

In the mid-eighties, Cal's heart deteriorated to the extent that he was placed on the waiting list for a heart transplant. "Waiting" it was, but he never wavered in his belief that his donor would appear in time.

Just when it appeared that time was about to run out, the beeper sounded on the pager he always carried with him. In 1987, Cal Stoll received his heart transplant. He later told me, "I still had the ball, but I was on my own one-yard line, and it was fourth down."

The transplant enabled Cal to live thirteen more years, until August of 2000. He filled those years by starting and guiding the Second Chance for Life Foundation, a volunteer group supporting those in need of transplants and promoting the unending demand for donors.

In these pages, I have covered Cal Stoll's Minnesota shut-out of Michigan, Kent Kitzmann's achievements under Stoll, the Gil Fash win over Illinois. There were many more big victories— UCLA, Washington, Michigan State (at East Lansing, where Cal had been an assistant coach), and other players— Rick Upchurch, John King, Tony Dungy, Michael Hunt, Marion Barber... but Cal Stoll's greatest victory, his greatest achievement, may well be The Second Chance for Life. With it, he moved upfield the full ninety-nine yards.

Joe and Ray

In late July in the early 1980s, Gopher head coach Joe Salem and I broadcast the State High School All-Star Football Game. The following week, I got a call from a listener, who told me that his German Shepherd dog gave birth to ten pups during the broadcast. Of the three male offspring, he named two of them "Joe" and "Ray."

I reported the blessed event on WCCO Radio and concluded with this tip to young would-be broadcasters:

"It's all in the delivery."

Hohensee's Biggest Game

In his two years at Minnesota, Mike Hohensee, a junior college transfer, established single-game and season records that still stand. His single-game records came in his finest game as a Gopher.

On November 7, 1981, Minnesota faced Ohio State at Memorial Stadium. The Buckeyes, a solid favorite, controlled the first half, building a 21-7 lead.

Early in the third quarter, Hohensee hit Jay Carroll with a 27-yard scoring pass. Less than three minutes later, he found Frank Jacobs on a 17-yard touchdown strike, and it was 21-21.

Ohio State bounced back, scoring near the end of the quarter to go back ahead, 28-21. A Buckeye field goal made it 31-21 with just over eight minutes to play.

Hohensee and Carroll teamed again with just under seven minutes left, an 18-yarder that made it 31-28.

The Gopher defense forced a punt, and Minnesota moved to the Ohio State 28. On third and ten, Hohensee aimed a pass at Carroll in the end zone. It was deflected, but Jay kept his focus and made the catch. Minnesota had upset Ohio State, 35-31.

Hohensee set two team records that still stand: 67 passes, 37 completions. The 444 passing yards and 5 touchdown passes were records at that time.

Chester Cooper was Mike's primary target in 1981 (60 receptions for 1,012 yards), but Jay Carroll had his big game. He caught only three passes that day, but all three were for touchdowns.

A trivia note: 1981 was the last year for Memorial Stadium, so Mike Hohensee was the quarterback in the Brickyard's finale, and in 1982, he quarterbacked the Gophers in their first year in the Metrodome.

Holtz To Gutekunst—A Quick Handoff

1985 was Lou Holtz's second and last year at Minnesota. The Gophers were 2-1 in non-conference games with the loss being their best effort. Against #1-ranked Oklahoma, Minnesota's defense was on the field for two-thirds of the game in a near-upset, a 13-7 loss to the Sooners. Linebacker Peter Najarian had 23 tackles.

In the Big Ten season, the Gophers began with a 45-15 win over Purdue. Ricky Foggie was 7 for 7 on passes for 212 yards.

The following Saturday, Minnesota topped Northwestern, 21-10. Foggie passed for 232 yards, 102 of them on three passes to tight end Kevin Starks.

The maroon and gold stayed unbeaten in the conference, with a 22-7 win in the rain at Indiana. This time, Foggie did not complete a pass, but the Gophers ran for 346 yards, 141 of them a career high for Valdez Baylor.

After close losses to Ohio State (23-19) and Michigan State (31-26), Minnesota bounced back with a 27-18 victory over Wisconsin. Foggie completed only five passes, but they totaled 242 yards, including an 89-yarder to Mel Anderson.

The regular season ended badly with decisive losses to Michigan (48-7) and Iowa (31-9). The Hawkeyes' triumph put them in the Rose Bowl.

The Gophers also managed to get a bowl bid. Despite a 4-4 finish in the Big Ten and a 6-5 record overall, they were chosen to play Clemson in the Independence Bowl.

That news was coupled with the resignation of Lou Holtz, who accepted an offer to coach at Notre Dame.

On December 5, Holtz's defensive coordinator, John Gutekunst, was named head coach. Gutie had just over two weeks to get the team ready for the Independence Bowl.

He did get the squad ready. On December 21, Minnesota scored the first ten points and the last ten points to defeat Clemson, 20-13. The Gophers' two touchdowns were textbook sustained drives. In the second quarter, the U of M went 91 yards on 13 plays. In the fourth quarter, it was 68 yards on 11 plays to break a 13-13 tie.

Free safety Donovan Small sealed the 20-13 win by breaking up two passes in the end zone. Named the game's defensive MVP, Small had eight tackles, an interception and a fumble recovery.

Five for Five

Free Safety Donovan Small was thrilled to be named the Most Valuable Defensive Player in Minnesota's 20-13 Independence Bowl win over Clemson in December of 1985.

Was that his biggest thrill? Probably not. As a high school junior in Wheeling, Illinois, Small took part in five consecutive plays, scoring on four of them. On the other play, he handled the ball twice and set up a score.

First, he ran over 80 yards for a touchdown.

Small kicked the extra point.

Then, Donovan kicked off, an onside kick.

It worked. Who recovered the ball? Small.

On the next play, he ran about 50 yards for another touchdown.

To conclude his string of five, he booted another extra point.

My Only Coaching Assignment

In 1986, my broadcast partner, Paul Flatley, and I were named the honorary coaches for the annual Spring Intra-Squad Football Game. Following the game, I got this nice letter from head coach John Gutekunst:

"On behalf of the University of Minnesota, we want to thank you for your participation in the 1986 Spring Football Game. Your coaching expertise was an integral part of our game plan, and I feel your input was reflected in the outcome of the game.

"Let me know if you ever want to make a career change to the coaching profession. We may not offer much in the way of job security, but we can offer you little pay for a lot of hard work."

What Gutie was kind enough not to mention was that my "coaching expertise input" was limited to choosing the opening play from scrimmage.

As I recall, it was a two-yard gain.

The Turn-Around Return

Sometimes a single play can turn a potential defeat into a rallying victory. I felt such a play was the key to a Minnesota win over Northwestern at the Metrodome October 11, 1986.

With 12 seconds to play in the first half, underdog North-western scored on a pass and extra point to take a 17-0 lead. Then came the comeback play. Mel Anderson took the kickoff on his 10-yard line and raced 90 yards. The extra point made it 17-7, and the Gopher squad charged to the locker room as if Minnesota had the lead.

In just over five minutes of the second half, the Gophers got the lead and went on to beat the Wildcats, 44-23. Darrell Thompson got most of his 176 yards and both his touchdowns in the second half, but the catalyst was Anderson's 90-yard return.

Lohmiller's Other 1986 Heroics

Chip Lohmiller's biggest last-second field goal was four weeks away, but on October 18, 1986, he had two last-second three-pointers.

Against Indiana, Lohmiller ended Minnesota's opening drive with a 56-yard field goal, at the time a team record.* Indiana rallied to take a 17-10 lead on a touchdown with one minute left in the first half. The Gophers got within range, and with three seconds left in the half, Chip boomed a 45-yarder to tighten the margin to 17-13.

In the second half, Darrell Thompson gained many of his 191 yards, and Lohmiller kicked a 27-yard field goal midway in the third quarter. 17-16 Indiana.

The Minnesota defense held the Hoosiers scoreless in the second half, and in the fourth quarter, Rickey Foggie's passing (he was 11 of 12 for the game) and Darrell's running brought Minnesota to chip-shot distance for Chip. With two seconds to play, Lohmiller kicked his fourth field goal of the day, a 21-yarder, and Minnesota had a 19-17 win.

* Later that same season, Lohmiller broke his own record with a mighty 62-yard field goal against Iowa. This time, though, the final-seconds heroics belonged to Rob Houghtlin of the Hawkeyes. His 37-yard field goal with one second remaining gave Iowa a 30-27 victory.

The Silence of the Wolverines

I am often asked, "What was your favorite game?" The Gil Fash game is covered in these pages. But that's not it. Neither is the 1999 win over Penn State, also found in this book. The year 2000 brought a 29-17 win over Ohio State at Columbus, meaning that now I had done the play-by-play of a Gopher football victory at every Big Ten city (the previous road win over Ohio State was in 1949). The 1977 shutout of Michigan, 16-0, was big- the #1-ranked Wolverines had gone 112 consecutive games without being blanked, but another victory over Michigan is at the top of my list.

My all-time favorite came in 1986 at Michigan Stadium. The Wolverines were solid favorites, but Minnesota was absolutely their equal. The score reflected that, 17-17 with about a minute to play. Gopher quarterback Rickey Foggie, unable to find an open receiver, took off on a zigzag 31-yard scramble that brought Minnesota within field goal range. The Gophers took some time off the clock on a play that put the ball where Chip Lohmiller wanted it. Lohmiller then split the uprights, and the clock read 0:00.

Now came the most beautiful moment of all. Over 100,000 Michigan fans sat in stunned silence, the most thrilling lack of sound I can ever remember.

Chip Lohmiller kicks another game-winner

The Game of Football

Football is the best team game I know. On any given offensive play, eleven men have specific roles to support the play, sometimes to create a distraction, a decoy, but always playing a role. On defense, it's more of a guessing game. If you guess wrong, quick reaction can still save the day. The defense can go on offense, too. That's how quarterback sacks are made.

Aside from the team element, there are two other things that distinguish football from all other sports.

One—the shape of the ball. In virtually all other sports, the ball is completely round. The football is an oval with pointed ends. You never know how it will bounce. We've all seen fumbles that caromed from hand to hand until somebody finally corralled the ball, and we've seen a good-looking punt that took a backward bounce or a bad-looking punt that took a forward bounce.

Two—the first down. A lightning-strike touchdown pass or run or kick return is exciting, but a score isn't needed to sustain interest, and on a third down drive, a string of first downs can sometimes beat a big-play opponent. If you have the ball, the opponent can't score.

Unless it has a defense that forces turnovers.

But that's another story.

Fireworks in the Fourth

On October 10, 1987, Minnesota met Northwestern at Evanston. The experts predicted a high-scoring game. Instead, the first half was a defensive struggle, with the Gophers leading at the intermission, 7-6.

The third quarter was all Minnesota, with the Gophers piling up 17 unanswered points.

The fourth quarter was all-offense, and the experts' high-scoring prediction came true in a big way. The Wildcats scored two touchdowns to make it 24-19 Minnesota. Then, Rickey Foggie hit Jason Bruce on an 80-yard lightning bolt. 31-19. Northwestern came right back, driving to another touchdown. 31-26. Darrell Thompson ran for 60 yards, and it was 38-26. Again, the Wildcats countered. 38-33. With just over a minute to play, Foggie broke loose for 71 yards and a 45-33 Gopher victory.

In that fourth quarter, Northwestern outscored Minnesota 27-21, but the Gophers' three touchdown plays totalled 211 yards, and that was enough for the win.

From the Field to the Booth

"Draw play and breaking into the open is Thompson. Cuts to the outside, goes out to the 15, to the twen—breaks into the clear! The 30, the 40, the 50, the 40, three men chasing. He is to the 20, he is to the 10, there are no flags, and he has scored a touchdown on a run of 98 yards!!"

There, verbatim, is my play-by-play of sophomore Darrell Thompson's record-setting run against Michigan on November 7, 1987. That recording is, by far, the most repeated of any single sports happening I have ever broadcast.

Darrell Thompson came to Minnesota from Rochester, Minnesota (John Marshall High School). His career totals, 1986 to 1989, still stand at the top of Gopher rushing statistics:

> 936 carries
> 4,654 yards
> 23 one hundred-yards-plus games
> 40 touchdowns

There are other rushing marks in which he shares the top spot: 4 touchdowns in a game, 13 in a season.

I was able to really get to know Darrell when he and Dave Mona shared Gopher broadcasts with me my final three years. Originally, Darrell was scheduled to work from the field, a difficult and unrewarding job for anyone, especially for a comparative newcomer to play-by-play. During our second game together, I brought Darrell into the booth with Dave and me. I told him, "We won't say you're down on the field, and we won't say you're here in the booth. We'll just do it."

It worked beautifully. Darrell has become a skilled broadcast professional and contributes mightily to the community as executive director of Bolder Options in the Twin Cities, working closely with young people whose lives could go up or down. Thanks to Darrell Thompson, the direction almost always is up.

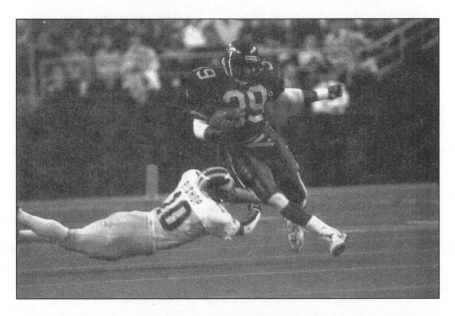

A clear field ahead-98 yards for Darrell Thompson

Dave Mona, Ray Christensen, Darrell Thompson

The Lumpkin Leap

Sean Lumpkin was a big-play defensive back for the Gophers, causing fumbles, recovering fumbles, intercepting passes and
making big tackles. I remember best a play Sean made that did not
win a game, but it sure prevented a loss.

On October 8, 1988, Minnesota scored three first-quarter
touchdowns. Northwestern scored three second-quarter touchdowns. 21-21 at the half. The Wildcats got seven more points in
the third quarter. The Gophers tied it in the fourth. Then Northwestern, on an effective two-minute offense, drove to the Minnesota 22-yard line with just enough time for a potential game-winning field goal. Lumpkin had other ideas. With a mighty leap, he
blocked Ira Adler's 39-yard attempt.

Since this game preceded the advent of college football
overtimes, the game ended a 28-28 tie.

The Upholsterer from Brooklyn

Mark Davy has worked with the University of Minnesota Men's Athletics Department for most of his life, most recently as Executive Director of the Men's M Club.

In the fall of 1988, Davy was an assistant athletic director at the University. A long distance call from Abie in Brooklyn, New York, was transferred to Mark.

Abie was eighty-three years old and a retired upholsterer. When he was a boy in Brooklyn, he and his friends each chose a favorite college football team and remained true to that team always. For some reason, Abie's father was attracted to the Minnesota Gophers. Accordingly, the Gophers became Abie's team. They were still his team. Their history was an integral part of Abie's life. Now he had heard that Memorial Stadium was being torn down. He wanted to see that stadium and walk on that field before it disappeared forever.

An appointment was made. Abie made the necessary arrangements, made the trip and met Mark.

Would they be able to get into the stadium? No problem. The dismantling had already begun.

They walked through the main gate (soon to be dismantled, brick by brick, and completely restored as a tilted Gateway inside the not-yet-constructed alumni center). The stadium turf was still intact. The two walked the length of the field.

During the walk, Abie looked everywhere, and, with reverence, spoke the names of Babe LeVoir, Bud Wilkinson, Sonny Franck, Leo Nomellini, Paul Giel... the names streamed forth, accompanied by the tears streaming down his face.

Abie had never seen a Gopher game, but he had heard countless Gopher games on his short-wave radio.

He had dreamed of this moment, and at age eighty-three, his dream had become real.

The Other Foggie

Quarterback Rickey Foggie ended his illustrious four years with the Gophers in 1987. That was the first year of play for his cousin, Fred Foggie. Fred did not letter that year but more than earned his "M" the next three.

In 1988, Fred Foggie played as a tailback and flanker. His junior year, he was moved to the other side of the ball, and as a cornerback, finished with two excellent seasons.

His most memorable play came on October 21, 1989, his senior year. Indiana, leading Minnesota 21-11, lined up for a short field goal. Frank Jackson knifed through to block the attempt; Foggie grabbed the ball at his 2-yard line and raced 98 yards the other way. In a ten-point turnaround, the Gophers now trailed by just 3 points instead of 13.

Unfortunately, the Hoosiers bounced back with a touchdown to win the game, 28-18, but Fred Foggie had placed himself in the U of M record book with the longest return of a blocked field goal.

Boomerang

Minnesota faced Utah in the opening game of the 1990 football season. The Utes shocked the Gophers with 19 unanswered points in the first quarter.

Then U of M quarterback Marquel Fleetwood took over, running and passing (for the game he had 85 yards passing and 69 rushing) to bring Minnesota to a 29-29 tie after three quarters.

With time running down, Minnesota's Drinon Mays blocked a Utah punt on the opposing 35. The Gopher offense worked the ball to the 11 and called time. In what was planned as the game-winning play to end the game, the field goal unit came on.

It was indeed the game-winner, but in the other direction. The center snap was bobbled, the low kick was blocked, and Utah's Lavon Edwards snared the ball and raced 91 yards for a touchdown.

Utah 35 - Minnesota 29.

I was amazed that the teflon ceiling of the Metrodome didn't collapse.

Thanks, Coach

On November 21, 1991, John Gutekunst announced his resignation as head football coach. Upon hearing that Gutekunst was leaving, one of the younger players left a letter on his desk. Gutie gave me permission to read it on the air, and I submit it again now to remind us of what coaching is all about.

"What's up, Coach? Nothing much here. Just trying to study some to make something of myself.

"I'll get to the point. I don't know if me writing this will mean much to you. But I will say this anyway.

"I know that times like this are hard for your family. But just hold on and be the strong man that you are. It really hurts me to see you leave when I just got here. If I never get to talk to you again, Coach, I just want to say thank you because you are the man who started it all for me. You didn't only give me a scholarship, but you may have saved my life and many others. If some of us had not received these opportunities, we might be at home now, running the dangerous streets that our parents tried to keep us out of. Now we are prospering young men who are trying to make something of themselves in a college environment. Thanks, Coach. You have my prayers and best wishes wherever you go from here. If I make it big or not, I will never forget you. You are the one that gave me the opportunity to crawl out of the hole."

The Proposal

The week of the final game of the 1992 season, against Iowa at the Metrodome, I received an e-mail request from Paul of St. Cloud. He was a University of Minnesota graduate; he and my son Jim had been in the U of M marching band together, and he and his girlfriend, Kim, would be at Saturday's game.

The request: Would I, on the air during the game, tell Kim that Paul wanted her to marry him?

I managed to insert the proposal (the only one during my fifty years of play-by-play) during a first-quarter time out. Sitting in the stands, a portable radio appropriately tuned, Kim heard it and said "Yes."

The Gophers, 1 and 9 going into the game, celebrated by knocking off Iowa, 28-13.

Coach Jim Wacker, happy to conclude his first Minnesota season with a victory, said I had his okay to be a marriage broker during every Gopher game in the future.

The Scoring Marathon

On October 9, 1993, Minnesota defeated Purdue 59-56, the highest point total for two teams in Gopher history. The Boilermakers were never behind until the final play of the third quarter, when Justin Conzemius intercepted a pass and ran 55 yards to give Minnesota a 49-42 lead. That was the only touchdown scored by either defense in the entire game.

Purdue tied the game in the fourth quarter, but Minnesota went back ahead, 56-49, with seven and a half minutes to play. The Boilers tied it again, on Mike Alstott's fifth touchdown of the game, with 2:06 on the clock.

The Gophers then drove to the Purdue one-yard line, and with eight seconds left, Mike Chalberg kicked an 18-yard field goal, the only field goal attempt in a game with sixteen touchdowns and sixteen extra points.

Other stats:

	Minnesota	Purdue
First downs	26	27
Rushing yards	223	299
Passing yards	402	260
Net total yards	625	559
Pass att/comp/int	36/24/1	25/16/3
Punts (yes, there were punts)	4/31.1	3/42.0
Fumbles/lost	1/1	4/1

Omar Douglas of the Gophers set a Big Ten record with five touchdown receptions. Scott Eckers threw six scoring passes in all. Mike Alstott rushed for four touchdowns and 171 yards and caught a pass for a fifth touchdown. Minnesota's Chris Darkins ran for 149 yards and a touchdown. Minnesota scored on nine of its fifteen possessions, Purdue on eight of its fifteen.

Purdue	14	14	14	14	56
Minnesota	7	14	28	10	59

One year later, at West Lafayette, there was another scoring marathon. This time, Purdue won it, 49-37. Chris Darkins ran for 234 yards for Minnesota; Mike Alstott had 183 yards rushing for the Boilermakers. The two teams totaled 1,165 yards, just 19 short of the 1993 total.

In 1995 came one more marathon. Minnesota scored on its last five possessions to win, 39-38. Cory Sauter found Ryan Thelwell on a two-point conversion with 1:38 to play. Purdue just missed a 42-yard field goal with 21 seconds left. Chris Darkins set a single-game Gopher record with 294 rushing yards. Total yardage, both teams: 1,007.

Total yardage, both teams, for 1993, 1994 and 1995: 3,356.

Dr. Ben

Dr. Frank Bencriscutto was the Director of Bands at the University of Minnesota from 1960 to 1992. Although his last name is pronounced ben-cris-SHOOT-oh, no one used it. He was "Dr. Ben" to everyone.

As composer, conductor and saxophone/clarinet soloist, his music had and continues to have a worldwide influence. When the Golden Gopher football team played in the Rose Bowl in 1961 and 1962, the University Marching Band came to the attention of football fans and marching band enthusiasts alike with its pregame and halftime performances. (See "The Band")

The band was on the move, not static. Its arrangements, in "big band" style, were sophisticated, complicated and very appealing. The performances were so well received that they led to great November concerts in the University's Northrop Auditorium.

Beyond his excellence in every phase of music-making, Frank Bencriscutto had an enthusiasm that swept everyone along with it.

The University of Minnesota Marching Band today numbers about 300. Under Jerry Luckhardt, it continues the musicianship and the spirit of Dr. Ben.

The Band

My son Jim was a member (tenor sax) of the University of Minnesota Marching Band for all of his five years at the U. My wife Ramona and I are well aware of the countless hours of practice band members put in, starting with Spat Camp, long before fall classes begin, and continuing throughout the season. Their practice hours approximate those of the football team. Like Jim, most of the band members are not music majors, but they are musical and they are enthusiastically devoted to what they do.

"What they do" dates back to 1892 when the cadet corps band, 29 strong, directed by engineering student Neville Staughton, began performing at Gopher football games. The band grew in importance and numbers, but did not have a full-time director until 1932 when Gerald Prescott began a 25-year tenure in that post. Through technique books and music arrangements for grade school, junior high and high school students, Prescott laid the basis for a pipeline, bringing students to the university and specifically to the University of Minnesota Marching Band.

Frank Bencriscutto, "Dr. Ben," Director of Bands from 1960 to 1992, created on-the-field techniques, cadences and choreography that you can see at Minnesota games and elsewhere today. Before the game, when you watch the band perform the "Swinging Gate" formation during the Battle Hymn of the Republic, that's Dr. Ben. (See "Dr. Ben.")

The University of Minnesota Marching Band

What do players think of the band? After all, they're in the locker room during the band's game day performances. In 1995, I was inducted into the Gopher Men's Sports Hall of Fame (in a special category—I was not a Gopher athlete). Judge Dickson, a fullback on the two Rose Bowl teams, was a fellow inductee. We stood next to each other during the halftime ceremony which honored the newest Hall of Fame members. When the band, formed immediately behind us, ended its piece, I looked up at Judge and saw a couple of tears rolling down his face. I cocked my head quizzically. He smiled and said, "I was okay until the band started playing."

Size Isn't Everything

Gopher All-American defensive back Tyrone Carter and wide receiver Tutu Atwell were both listed at 5-feet-9-inches tall. (I always suspected Tyrone was 5-8.) On September 21, 1996, in a game in which they were two of the shortest players on the field,

Tyrone Carter—a fumble recovery and a
touchdown—twice in this game

they led the Gophers to a 35-33 upset of a ranked Syracuse team. In the third quarter, Carter picked up a fumble and ran 63 yards for a score. Less than a minute later, he grabbed another fumble and carried it in from the Syracuse 20, setting an NCAA single-game record.

Atwell caught six passes for 126 yards, including a 50-yard touchdown throw from Cory Sauter.

Adam Bailey's 26-yard field goal with 42 seconds on the clock gave the Gophers their 35-33 win.

Bailey was listed at 5'10".

As I say, size isn't everything.

Homecoming

Over my 50 years of Gopher football, two University of Minnesota homecoming games stand out.

In 1978 at Memorial Stadium, underdog Indiana shocked the Gophers early by building a 24-0 lead, with two of the touchdowns coming on a long pass and a long fumble return. Not until late in the second quarter did the Gophers break the scoring drought when Marion Barber ended a drive with a touchdown plunge. He did the same for the only score of the third quarter. In the fourth quarter, however, Indiana retaliated to make it 31-14. Then, with nine and a half minutes to play, Wendell Avery, who had come off the bench, hit Roy Artis with a 14-yard scoring pass. Minnesota got the ball back, and Avery found Elmer Bailey on a 19-yard scoring pass. 3:04 to play. Avery completed a two-point conversion pass to Bailey, and it was 31-29 Hoosiers. The Gophers forced Indiana to punt, and Avery led a hurry-up drive to within field goal range. With two seconds to play, Paul Rogind calmly kicked a 31-yarder, and it was happy homecoming for the U of M.

The other big homecoming comeback was at the Metrodome against favored Michigan State in 1998. Minnesota had lost seventeen in a row to the Spartans. When State recovered quarterback Andy Persby's fumble in the end zone for a safety, the visitors led 18-10. With just under ten minutes remaining, loss number 18 appeared imminent.

However, Minnesota's defense stopped Michigan State, and Billy Cockerham came in to lead a drive that ended with a 24-yard touchdown pass to Luke Leverson (in the first quarter, Leverson returned a punt for 68 yards and a score). With 1:47 to play, Cockerham's two-point conversion pass to Leverson failed. The subsequent on-side kickoff by Adam Bailey did not fail. Craig Scruggs leaped high to snare the ball on the Minnesota 47. Two plays later, on third and 15, Cockerham scrambled all the way to the Michigan State 23 to set up Bailey's winning field goal with just 13 seconds left.

The final: Minnesota 19 - Michigan State 18.

My Top Twenty-two in Football

Football is such a body-to-body team game that it's often very difficult to isolate standout players, especially on defense. I've done the best my memory permits. This team dates from 1951 through 2000, my fifty years of Golden Gopher football broadcasts.

These are listed in the order they first lettered:

Paul Giel (Back-'51) Mr. Everything. Run, pass, punt, kick return, interceptor

Bob McNamara (Back-'51) Outstanding two-way player, plus kick returns

Bob Hobert (Tackle-'54) Fierce and intelligent

Tom Brown (Lineman-'58) Outland Trophy, destroyed opponents' offense-defense

Judge Dickson (Back-'59) Rarely thrown for a loss

Sandy Stephens (QB-'59) Skilled quarterback with an incredible will to win

Bobby Bell (Lineman-'60) Outland Trophy, could have played any position

Aaron Brown (End-'63) Tough on defense, good receiver on offense

Jeff Wright (Def back-'68) Uncanny sense for the ball, great interceptor

Bill Light (Linebacker-'69) Superb tackler, team leader

Rick Upchurch (Back-'73) He had two speeds. "Fast" was the slower gear

Mike Hohensee (QB-'81) A brilliant, scrambling passer

Pete Najarian (Linebacker-'82) Tackle leader all four years

Rickey Foggie (QB-'84) Time and again, he made things happen

Chip Lohmiller (Place-kicker-'84) 57 field goals, and he beat Michigan in '86

Ron Johnson- a fingertip catch against Iowa

Darrell Thompson (Back-'86) Good speed, great determination

Sean Lumpkin (Def back-'88) Great instincts, rarely fooled

Aaron Osterman (Receiver-'92) My favorite third down go-to guy

Tutu Atwell (Receiver/kick ret-'94) His size (5'9") never held him back

Tyrone Carter (Def back-'96) In practice, on game day, always the best tackler

Ben Hamilton (Center-'97) A model for all high school centers

Ron Johnson (Receiver-'98) Size (6'3"), strength, unwavering focus

On Broadcasting a Game

There are many different ways to broadcast a football or basketball game, no one right way. I have always felt that the radio play-by-play person is providing the basic ingredients, enabling the listener to paint his or her own picture. The more accurate that picture, the better the broadcaster has done the job. At the same time, the announcer does not need to give every little detail. Let the listener embellish the image as desired. If that image becomes one of the broadcaster and not the game, then the listener has been misled.

The spot of the ball, the down and yards to go, the switch to a zone, the length of a jump shot, the score (we all fail to give the score often enough)—these are essential. Stories of players and coaches, historical anecdotes—these have their place, but not when they interfere with the action on the field or court.

Television may use the excuse that the viewer has a picture, thereby giving license to the telecasters to ignore the action while relating an "entertaining" or "humorous" anecdote. This is true only to a limited extent.

Give the game itself its due, Announcer. It's been around a lot longer than you, and it will still be around when you're gone.

Images

In recent years, perhaps no single image has become more indelibly etched in the minds of University of Minnesota football fans than the game-winning field goal that gave the Gophers a 24-23 upset of second-ranked Penn State at Beaver Stadium November 6, 1999 (see "The Field Goal and the Fans").

It turned the Minnesota football program around, and because of national, state and local media coverage, almost everyone got to "see" it.

First, the quiet before the kick. Penn State calls a time out to try to unsettle freshman kicker Dan Nystrom. The image is of Nystrom, still three months away from his nineteenth birthday, kneeling, trying to focus, trying to shut out everything but what he has to do.

Now, the kick. The stadium noise swells. The snapper is Derek Rackley, one of the best snappers in Gopher history. His snap is not up to his usual high standards. Holder Ryan Rindels does an effective job of fielding the ball and putting it down, but it delays the kick a split second. There is the image of soaring Penn State players (one of them LaVar Arrington, a field goal-blocking specialist). They have timed their leaps to coincide with a perfectly executed field goal attempt. The split-second delay means they are starting to come down from the apex of their jump when Nystrom's kick takes off and sails through the uprights. (Assistant Athletics Director Marc Ryan watched the film several times and was able to verify that sequence.)

Now, the image of the entire Gopher sideline rushing onto the field in wild celebration.

All but one man.

Athletics Director Mark Dienhart stays rooted for a few seconds, then goes on to the field.

A little later, Ryan asks Dienhart about his sideline hesitation. Dienhart, who has seen the Gophers come so close so often, explains, "I wanted to be sure there weren't any flags."

The Field Goal and the Fans

On November 6, 1999, Minnesota upset highly-rated Penn State at Beaver Stadium, 20-17, on freshman Dan Nystrom's game-ending field goal. The kick was set up by a pass from Billy Cockerham, intended for Ron Johnson but deflected into the arms of another Gopher receiver, Arland Bruce. It was an alert play by Bruce but admittedly a fortunate bounce for Minnesota.

Penn State fans could have taken refuge in the "you were lucky" theme. Instead, as our three team buses left (we had to go around three sides of Beaver Stadium to get to the exit road), Penn State fans waved to us; some even applauded. A few just stood there, which was fine, and no one gave us "the finger." It was class personified.

I'll never forget the deflected pass to Bruce and Nystrom's field goal. Neither will I forget the Penn State fans and their sportsmanship.

Changes

A frequent question I get, after fifty years of play-by-play, is, "How has the game changed?" My answer is focused on basketball and football, by far my principal sports through those years.

For me, basketball has changed more than football. With only a few exceptions, teams have become more up-tempo, more pressure-oriented. The emphasis on the big men has declined. Now the guards are more likely to be the key to a team's success. Defense has become increasingly important—the transition basket has climbed in the statistics. The shot clock has stepped up the flow of the game. The three-point basket has helped spread the offense. As part of that spread, there are more and more tall forwards and a few centers shooting and making the threes. Because of the increased intensity of play, the offensive and defensive pressure, nine or ten players usually get significant minutes of playing time. In my early years, a team could get by with six or seven. Not any more.

Football has had its changes too. In my early years, the platoon system came in, was dropped, then brought back. The play clock, the two-point conversion, overtime—all have been added. The biggest change may not be in the rules but rather in the size, power and agility of the players. They are bigger, stronger and quicker. There were no soccer-style kickers when I began. Now the kicking game threatens to take over the sport. Too many kick-offs into the end zone or out of it, too many field goals, have taken away some of the excitement. On the other side of the equation, the defense has become a more integral part of football, sometimes gambling but always exciting. Fans now talk defense almost as much as they do offense. And football remains a remarkable "team" sport-eleven men trying to function as a single unit. When they do, it's a thrilling achievement.

The Hall of Fame

On August 11, 2000, I was presented the Chris Schenkel Award, given to one person each year "for excellence in college football broadcasting." The award in itself is an honor I never dreamed of. To be included in the College Football Hall of Fame is a feeling beyond words.

The Hall began at Kings Island, Ohio. It was moved to its brand new home in South Bend, Indiana, effective August 25, 1995. The building is in downtown South Bend, next to the city's convention center. The exterior resembles a football stadium. One of the rooms inside is a mini-stadium, complete with the sound of a roaring crowd.

A feature that intrigues me is the circular ramp that winds down inside the museum. Exactly 100 yards in length, it follows the theme "Pursuit of a Dream," representing the stages of a football-wannabe child to the actual college football hero.

Exhibits cover a wide range—actual footballs through the years, equipment through the years, a variety of films and other pictorials, recorded college marching bands (no University of Minnesota Marching Band, but then, no museum is perfect), several "hands-on" exhibits appealing to all ages, and much more.

Most impressive of all, though, are the life castings of the faces of each enshrined player or coach. The casting is displayed for the first time at the banquet at which that person is inducted into the hall, then placed at the person's niche in the museum.

Sixteen University of Minnesota players and coaches are enshrined:

End and kicker Ed Rogers (1901-03), end Bobby Marshall (1904-06), quarterback John McGovern (1908-10), end Bert Baston (1914-16), fullback Herb Joesting (1925-27), fullback and tackle Bronko Nagurski (1927-29), coach Fritz Crisler (1930-31), halfback Francis "Pug" Lund (1932-34), coach Bernie Bierman (1932-41, 1945-50), tackle Ed Widseth (1934-36), halfback Bruce Smith (1939-41), tackle Dick Wildung (1940-42), center Clayton Tonnemaker (1946-49), tackle and guard Leo Nomellini (1947-49), halfback Paul Giel (1951-53), and tackle Bobby Bell (1960-62).

Pay them a visit.

From the College Football Hall of Fame,
Paul Giel's life casting image

Completing the Cycle

In 1949, Minnesota shut out Ohio State at Columbus, 27-0. Wes Fesler was the Buckeye head coach.

I began broadcasting U of M football in 1951. Wes Fesler was the new Gopher head coach.

Though admittedly there was a span of thirteen years during which the teams did not play, I never did the play-by-play of a Minnesota victory at Columbus in my first forty-nine years.

That finally ended October 14, 2000, at Ohio Stadium. Minnesota jumped into a 17-3 lead in the first quarter and never looked back. It was a decisive victory.

Rushing yards	138-70 for Minnesota
Passing yards	243-130 for Minnesota
First downs	22-13 for Minnesota
Final score	29-17 for Minnesota

I had now broadcast a Gopher victory at every Big Ten school's home field.

In the postgame interview with Glen Mason, I had trouble expressing myself. I was literally choked with emotion. Coach Mason understood completely. He said he felt the same way. This win, against the school he played for and coached for, was a major step forward for his program at Minnesota.

Network television and radio also were kind enough to share my joy with in-game and postgame coverage.

The Jacket from South Korea

In April of 2001, I received an incredible gift from a Gopher fan, originally from Wayzata, Minnesota, now living in Inchon, South Korea. He had met me just once, and only briefly, but was a solid supporter of Minnesota sports and of my broadcasts.

Early Sunday morning, October 15, 2000, in Inchon, he got on the internet and picked up the entire second half of the Minnesota-Ohio State game. Minnesota won that game, my only victory ever at Ohio Stadium. He was thrilled by it, and that led him to order a jacket made for me, the gift that arrived the following April.

It's made of a soft leather, beautifully tailored. The lettering is in gold on a maroon background. On the left front, as I wear the jacket, from top to bottom, one word to a line, are the one-inch words: RAY/"THE VOICE OF THE GOPHERS"/ CHRISTENSEN. On the right front, top to bottom: a four-inch head of Goldy Gopher, then OCT 14/2000/MINNESOTA/29 OHIO STATE/17.

The back has MINNESOTA in three-and-a-half-inch letters, forming an arch over a seven-and-a-half-inch block M. Below that, in 2-inch letters, GOLDEN GOPHERS.

The gift was sent to my downtown WCCO Radio office. I called Ramona and described it. She was appreciative but then asked, "Where are you going to wear it?"

She was right, of course. Wearing the jacket would hardly be unobtrusive.

We are thrilled with the jacket, I have found special occasions to wear it, and it is displayed prominently with my memorabilia.

Color Commentators

"Analysts" is a more accurate word, but somehow, "color" is the word applied most often to the men and women who bring flesh to the bones of play-by-play.

I have been blessed with a succession of knowledgeable men in my Gopher football broadcasts (Carole Kerner was the only woman analyst to work with me, but not for U of M games. She was excellent).

Photo by Ramona Christensen

The Jacket from South Korea

Al Gowans, a high school head coach, and former Gopher lineman George Svendsen, worked as a pair with me. They often disagreed, always convincingly and always respectful of each other.

Paul Giel and Billy Bye, both former Gopher halfbacks, were similar in style and personality. They were fun to be with, on and off the air, but we never let our fun interfere with the game.

Murray Warmath and Cal Stoll, both former Gopher coaches, never rested on their credentials. They came to every game completely prepared.

Paul Flatley and I worked together for fifteen years. Earlier, I had done the play-by-play when Paul's Northwestern team defeated Minnesota, largely because of Paul's uncanny knack for catching passes on hook patterns. Our years together were productive and satisfying.

In my final three years, I returned to having two analysts, Dave Mona, a public relations executive, and former Gopher Darrell Thompson (Darrell's 98-yard touchdown run is the most-played of my Gopher highlights tapes). Dave and I share a similar sense of humor. Aside from that, Dave "sees" the field extremely well, and he is no stranger to broadcasting. Darrell started with very little broadcast experience but has quickly become a very good partner. The two of them have joined Dave Lee (my play-by-play successor) to form the new Gopher football broadcast team.

I have always worked Gopher basketball games by myself. I started that way, and somehow it never changed. My youngest son, Jim, was with me for the last 25 years and over 500 football and basketball games. Jim kept individual and other statistics and often saw things I missed. He was my right hand for home games and some special postseason games. He "retired" when I did but kept his day job.

A highlight through all these years was the national anthem. All of us, Jim, analysts, technician and me, stood, faced the flag and sang. That will be a lasting memory.

A note on superstition. I would wear the same jacket and tie on a road trip if the Gophers had come home with a win the trip before—things like that, but rarely anything more.

Ray and son Jim at Ray's final football broadcast,
December 27, 2000, the Micronpc.com Bowl

The most complete bow to superstition came with Dave, Darrell and me. Before a game, I accidentally spilled coffee on some of my papers, and Dave found a penny in the broadcast booth. The Gophers rallied to win.

Before the next game, under controlled conditions with paper toweling ready, I spilled coffee on my papers. All of us touched Dave's penny.

The Gophers lost.

Biggest Disappointments

I have tried through fifty years of University of Minnesota football and forty-five of Gopher basketball not to let great victories send me to another planet nor to let unexpected losses drop me too many levels.

Two football defeats, though, stayed with me for several days rather than several hours.

In 1989, against Ohio State, Sean Lumpkin grabbed a quarterback fumble in midair and ran 85 yards for a touchdown. Minnesota had a 10-0 lead after one quarter. Three more scores made it 31-0 late in the second quarter, and Ohio State had to punt. Unfortunately, the Gophers had twelve men on the field. The Buckeyes got a first down instead, marched the length of the field, and scored with ten seconds left.

It was still 31-8 starting the second half, but the momentum had shifted. Ohio State outscored Minnesota 33-6, with the winning touchdown coming with 57 seconds to play. 41-37 Ohio State, and Minnesota had blown a 31-0 lead.

The other painful football loss came December 27, 2000, my 510th and last gridiron play-by-play, in the Micronpc.com Bowl in Fort Lauderdale, Florida.

In our pregame broadcast, my on-air partners, Dave Mona and Darrell Thompson, picked Minnesota to win. I went with North Carolina State. In less than two minutes, the Gophers had intercepted a pass on the Wolfpack 28 and gone on to score. In the same quarter, Minnesota scored on drives of 74 and 72 yards. At the end of the quarter, the Gophers had 222 yards on offense and a 21-0 lead. Midway in the second quarter, a field goal made it 24-0.

During the commercial break that followed the field goal, Darrell and Dave asked me if I wanted to change my pick. On the theory that you're never wrong until the final score proves you're wrong, I said no.

The final score proved I was right. North Carolina State scored late in the first half, then added two touchdowns and a field goal in the third quarter to make it 25-24 for the Wolfpack. The Gophers got the lead back on Dan Nystrom's field goal, but State scored another touchdown less than a minute later and went on to win, 38-30.

Tellis Redmon ran for 246 yards for Minnesota, but the Gopher defense could not protect a 24-0 lead, and my final football broadcast was a major disappointment.

In basketball disappointments, one game stands out. On January 25, 1972, Minnesota and Ohio State met at Williams Arena. Bill Musselman's Gophers were 4-0 in the Big Ten, the Buckeyes 3-0.

In the final seconds of the first half, Ohio State missed a shot, keeping the score at 23-23. Gopher guard Bobby Nix raised his fist, happy about the missed shot. As Nix headed toward the locker room, the Buckeyes' seven-foot center Luke Witte elbowed Nix in the head. Television replays clearly showed Nix's head jolted backward by the blow.

In the second half, Ohio State established a 50-44 lead with less than a minute to play. Witte drove to the basket. Clyde Turner blocked him to the floor, was called for an intentional foul and was ejected from the game. Corky Taylor reached out to pull Witte up, but then kneed him in the groin. Ron Behagen, who had fouled out earlier, left the bench and attacked Witte. Other fights broke out, some with fans participating. When order finally was restored, Athletics Director Paul Giel announced that the game was over (the clock showed 36 seconds remaining), and Ohio State was the winner.

I described all of this as it happened and stated flatly that Minnesota was the aggressor in a mugging. Witte was not blameless, but there still was no real excuse for what happened. Gopher fans in the stands booed, and I was convinced then, and still am, that they booed the violence, that this ugliness had no place in a college arena.

The Big Ten suspended Taylor and Behagen for the rest of the season. With two of its key players gone, the Gopher "Iron Five" (Turner, Nix, Dave Winfield, Jim Brewer and Keith Young) went on to win the Big Ten championship with an 11-3 record.

What I remember most keenly, though, is not the championship, but the way the January 25 game came to an end.

"The Use of Intoxicating Liquor—"

For over fifty years, Jules Perlt was the public address voice for University of Minnesota football and basketball games. His stentorian, "The use of intoxicating liquor in this stadium is strictly prohibited!" would reverberate throughout Memorial Stadium before every Gopher football game. Fans with fond memories still try to mimic the line today. But not very well. There was only one Julie.

Beneath the somewhat stern demeanor lay a mischievous nature. From time to time, Perlt would give other Big Ten scores. If Gopher fans were hoping Michigan would lose and the Wolverines did lose, Julie would tantalize them:

"Here is a final score:
Michigan 21 (pause)
Illinois 28!"

The stadium would erupt.

Perlt was a keen observer of all that made up a Gopher game. Once during pregame warmups, seated at the center court at Williams Arena, he beckoned a maintenance man.

"You'd better check that backboard support. One of the bolts must be loose."

The maintenance man got tools and ladder, discovered that a bolt indeed was loose, tightened it, climbed down, then hurried over to Perlt.

"How did you know, Julie?"

Perlt's calm reply: "It didn't sound right."

Basketball

The Game of Basketball

I have often been asked "What's your favorite sport to broadcast?" My answer has usually been "Whatever sport is coming up next on my broadcast schedule."

If I really had to narrow my answer to one sport, it would be basketball. The game is the ideal length. I can go full tilt for two hours, and if it's an overtime game, that in itself produces plenty of adrenaline. I have always worked Gopher basketball alone. The breaks in the action are usually filled with commercials. In football, I have been blessed with a remarkable group of analyst partners, but four and a half to five hours of broadcasting (including one hour pregame and half an hour postgame) is still a long time.

Basketball has a rhythm and grace that make it special. The shot clock, the three-point field goal and the alternate possession on a held ball have been positive additions. The really good player must play offense and defense and must make good moves with or without the ball. True, some games lose their rhythm by an endless parade to the free throw line, but these are the exception, not the rule.

For me, even a one-sided Gopher loss has its points of interest. Usually someone wearing the maroon and gold is having a double-figure game in scoring or rebounds.

In football, players are so layered with equipment (all of it necessary) that they become more a uniform than a person.

In basketball, you can see them sweat, and with each drop from the chin, the broadcast listener comes closer and closer to the action. Bringing my listener to the game has always been a major objective for me.

"I Hate the Twin Cities"

Ed Kalafat was an outstanding high school athlete in Anaconda, Montana. When he was given the chance to play basketball at the University of Minnesota, Ed had his doubts. His father convinced him to at least visit the Twin Cities.

He did. It was cold. It seemed colder than Anaconda. Worse than that, the Twin Cities were big. Anaconda had a population of 12,000. Ed came back home, reporting, "I hate the Twin Cities. I don't want to go to the University of Minnesota."

Fortunately, Ed's father had the last word.

Ed Kalafat came to Minnesota. Fellow players, led by Glen Reed, made him feel more at home, and he stayed.

Kalafat led Ozzie Cowles's team in scoring and free throw shooting in 1951-52. He was the team's top rebounder the next two years. Ed was named the Gophers' Most Valuable Player in 1954 and finished with a career scoring average of 14.5.

After graduation, he played with John Kundla's Minneapolis Lakers, then had a long and successful career as a banker.

Retired in Florida, Ed Kalafat still gets back to the Twin Cities periodically, and, yes, he enjoys it.

The Bridge Is Out

In December of 1959, the basketball team and I were on the last leg of a flight from a game at Vanderbilt to a game at Nebraska. The carrier was Frontier Airlines; the airplane was the venerable but reliable DC-3. For reason of limited pressurizing, the DC-3 flew at fairly low altitudes, and with its small size, lacked an intercom system. This final leg, to Lincoln, had one stop on the way at Beatrice, Nebraska.

As we neared Beatrice, the stewardess stood up at the front of the plane and announced, "We will not be landing at Beatrice because the bridge is out." Then she sat down.

Now, you don't hear that too often at 10,000 feet, so I inquired aloud as to whether she could explain the non landing in a little greater detail.

It turned out that there was only one road to the Beatrice airport, and heavy flooding had taken out a bridge on that road. Thus, no passengers or mail could get to or from the airport.

The announcement remains my No. 1 in-flight entertainment.

104... Not Always Enough

On January 8, 1962, at Williams Arena, John Kundla's Minnesota team defeated Indiana in a thriller, 104-100. Nineteen days later, at Bloomington, the Gophers reached the 104 mark again, but this time they lost, 105-104.

The difference was slightly-built (like a rail) Hoosier Jimmy Rayl, who set a school record that he still holds, 56 points.

In the overtime, Tom McGrann had all eleven Minnesota points, including two free throws that gave the Gophers a one-point lead with seven seconds to play. That was enough time for Rayl to hit another of his long jumpers, and the Hoosiers won.

Less than a month later, Rayl again scored 56 points, this time without the benefit of overtime, in a 113-94 victory over Michigan.

All this before the three-point shot.

The Transformation

As a high school star at Minneapolis South, Eric Magdanz had "soft hands." In his first year at Minnesota, Magdanz was a changed player, anything but relaxed. This has happened to a lot of players trying to make the transition from high school to the Big Ten. Some never succeed. Magdanz did succeed, in a big way.

Eric's second year, 1962, was a complete turn-around. The "old" Magdanz was back, the soft hands were back, and he became the "go-to" guy.

The "go-to" reached its peak in the season finale against Michigan at Ann Arbor. Magdanz broke George Kline's single-game scoring record of 40 points, set five years earlier. With 30 points in the second half, Magdanz, for the game, shot 16 of 25 from the field, made all ten of his free throws for a total of 42 points, and also grabbed 18 rebounds in a 102-80 win.

Nine years later, in the final home game of 1971, Ollie Shannon equaled Eric's 42 in a 104-98 victory over Wisconsin.

That 42-points mark still stands.

Lou Hudson

It's extremely difficult to name one favorite Gopher basketball player above all the others in a forty-five year span, but I settled on Lou Hudson several years ago, and I haven't changed my mind.

Freshmen were not eligible during Hudson's Minnesota years, but in his three varsity years (1963-64, 64-65 and 65-66), Lou averaged 20.4 points a game. In his senior year, in a game at Creighton, he broke a bone in his right wrist (his shooting hand) and missed seven games. Wearing a cast, he returned for the final thirteen games. Adjusting to left-handed shooting hurt his scoring but not his rebounding (the cast became a formidable weapon. After the season, the NCAA outlawed that type of hard cast). His defense was as good as ever. In fact, I think Hudson may have been a better defensive player than offensive, and that's saying a lot.

The broken wrist was a long-range blessing for Lou. It forced him to develop a left-handed shot. He became the first Gopher ever to be chosen in the first round of the NBA draft (4th pick) and went on to a very successful pro career with the St. Louis (later the Atlanta) Hawks. As a pro, he was almost impossible to defend because he could score equally well with left or right hand.

Lou Hudson with another rebound

Necessity Is the Mother of Invention

On December 23, 1968, the Gophers played at San Diego State. When the team arrived at the university's arena for a middle-of-the-day shoot-around, all doors were locked. There was no access to the basketball court, much less to any basketballs. University personnel had apparently begun their Christmas holiday.

The squad did have plenty of tape. There were outdoor bathrooms nearby. Coach Bill Fitch had his players raid the bathrooms for enough toilet paper for two basketball-sized spheres. Trainer Lloyd "Snapper" Stein wrapped both securely with tape. Then, in the parking lot, the Gophers went through a vigorous and enjoyable passing drill (no dribbling).

That night, the team was relaxed, the passing was efficient, and the Gophers won, 73-60.

Bill Fitch on Recruiting

Bill Fitch, the Gopher basketball coach in 1968-69 and 69-70, was a good recruiter, with an Irish wit and charm that usually not only put the potential recruit at ease but also impressed the player's mother.

Fitch told me this story, almost certainly untrue, about his recruiting effectiveness while at Minnesota. He went after four young men and was welcomed into their homes by the recruits and their mothers.

The four recruits wound up at Maryland, North Carolina State, Notre Dame and UCLA.

The four mothers all enrolled at the University of Minnesota.

The Warmup Show

Bill Musselman came to Minnesota in 1971. With one returning starter, Jim Brewer, Musselman led the Gophers to the Big Ten title, although the season was marred by an ugly finish to a game with Ohio State (see "Biggest Disappointments").

Musselman brought the crowds back to Williams Arena by 1) winning games and 2) his pregame warmup show.

The shows were led by George Schauer, who came with Musselman from Ashland College in Ohio. Schauer hardly ever saw game action, but he led his teammates in a clever ball-handling routine that Musselman started at Ashland. Done to the theme song "Sweet Georgia Brown," the routine definitely had a strong Harlem Globetrotter resemblance.

Another Musselman innovation dealt with the introduction of the Gopher starting lineup. In the darkened arena, the only illumination was a spotlight shining on each player as he charged through the center opening of a wooden cutout of a seventeen-foot high Gopher.

Not everyone liked the showbiz atmosphere, but it brought people back to the Barn, and they've been coming ever since.

The Fast Break

In the 1975-76 and 76-77 seasons, Ray Williams and Osborne Lockhart were a dynamic duo for the maroon and gold. They loved the game of basketball, especially when it went uptempo.

Flip Saunders was the point guard and controlled the half-court offense, but in the sudden transition offense, forward Williams and guard Lockhart took over. Their fast break usually contained a couple of passes each, but these were a blur, and if the two ever blew a fast-break basket, I don't remember it.

When Ray Williams was inducted into the Gopher Men's Sports Hall of Fame in November of 2001, he claimed (with a smile) that Lockhart, on a two-on-one fast break, was inclined to pull up for a twenty-to-thirty-foot jump shot.

I don't remember that either, and Ray, I'm inclined not to believe it.

The Best Opposing Team, the Best Opposing Player

In my forty-five years of basketball, I saw many outstanding teams play the Gophers. I feel that the best was Indiana's 1976 national champion team. The Hoosiers went unbeaten in 32 games, defeating an excellent Michigan team for the NCAA title. Indiana's starting lineup included forwards Scott May and Tom Abernethy, center Kent Benson and guards Quinn Buckner and Bob Wilkerson.

May and Benson were among the finest opposing players I ever described, but the number-one performer, for me, has to be Earvin "Magic" Johnson. He had the ability to turn a game around all by himself. In his two years at Michigan State in the late 70s, the Spartans won all four games against the Gophers. In 1978, he turned two seeming Minnesota victories into losses, 87-83 and 71-70. He was truly an amazing athlete, with a true love for the game.

The Bottomless Cup

At Crisler Arena at the University of Michigan, I always used to have a cup of coffee before the Minnesota-Michigan game. On this occasion, the coffee was incredibly strong. In the field of broadcasting, one becomes tolerant of a wide range of flavors and strengths of coffees, but this was not drinkable. I told the woman in charge of the media room that someone might have inadvertently doubled the amount, that it was much too strong.

She said, "Let me try it," grabbed a styrofoam cup and started to fill it.

So help me, the bottom fell out of the cup.

She looked at the splashed coffee and the flat circle of styrofoam at her feet, then looked at me and said, "That's strong."

A Memorable Title Game

On March 6, 1982, Minnesota and Ohio State met in the final game of the Big Ten regular season. Jim Dutcher's Gophers, 13-4, could take the Big Ten championship outright with a win. The Buckeyes, 12-5, could grab a share of the title with a win.

17,378 Williams Arena fans saw a championship performance by both teams, but the Gophers would not be denied. They shot 69.6 percent from the field in the first half, 66.7 percent in the second half. The Ohio State forwards, Clark Kellogg and Tony Campbell, scored 20 and 21 points respectively, but the maroon and gold guards and center controlled the game.

From the outside, the two guards, Trent Tucker and Darryl Mitchell, played all but one minute. Tucker scored 23 points. Mitchell ran the team and had 6 assists and 2 steals. Junior center Randy Breuer took care of the inside. Breuer started on the bench only because coach Jim Dutcher used the traditional "seniors" starting lineup for the final home game of the season. Randy came in after three minutes, played 36 minutes and scored 32 points.

Minnesota outscored Ohio State by six points in each half, led all the way, and wound up with an 87-75 victory. The Buckeyes played very well, but the Golden Gophers turned in one of the most complete forty-minute performances I ever described.

The Ups and Downs of Play-by-Play

On February 9, 1984, I left my sixth-floor room at the Holiday Inn on the Ohio State campus, ready to broadcast the Minnesota-Ohio State game. The St. John Arena was just one block away. It took me forty-five minutes to get there.

From the sixth floor, the elevator started its descent smoothly, then abruptly shuddered a few times before grinding to a stop, four feet below the doors of the second floor.

When pushing the first floor button several times produced nothing, I opened the little door marked "Telephone." There it was- the telephone cord, and nothing more.

Next I pushed the alarm button a few times, then discovered that pulling the red emergency button out kept the alarm ringing constantly, without my having to do anything else. The alarm was very loud in the elevator. I assumed it was at least a considerable annoyance outside the elevator.

Now. What does one do, trapped in an elevator?

First, take charge. Keep your fellow passengers calm. This was not too difficult since I was alone.

Second, remember that there is more air near the floor. I decided I was in no danger and remained standing.

I could see no way to escape through the roof of the car, as I remembered seeing in the movies, but then I was only four feet below a floor, so that was really not a consideration.

What remained was the pressure of time. When would I get out? It was a good thing I always left early for a game, but then, if I had left later, I'd be there, and someone else would be stranded in my elevator.

After ten minutes that seemed much longer, a workman called out, "We're here!" I turned off the alarm and shouted that I had a basketball game to broadcast, in the hope that would help.

I could hear the two of them prying at the doors. The doors opened an inch or two, then slid shut once more. Now one of the men began pounding at the doors. There was probably some reason for this, but I kept thinking, "I can pound from my side while you do something more productive out there."

Then, suddenly, quietly, smoothly, the doors slid open. I handed up my attache case, then got pulled up to the second floor. One of the men said, "The other two elevators are working." I replied, "I'll walk."

Minnesota lost the game, 73-62, but the pregame was far more dramatic than usual.

The Madison Story

There are incidents in athletics that one would like to forget but cannot. However, there seems to be a pattern in athletics that something reassuring often follows a negative happening.

On January 23, 1986, the Gophers won a thrilling 67-65 game at Wisconsin. In those days, I made my own travel arrangements, so I was back in the Twin Cities the following day when I learned that three Gopher players had been charged with rape. Two were arrested at the airport as the team was preparing to leave Madison. Later, a third was taken into custody.

The three players, all starters, were eventually acquitted, but their basketball careers at Minnesota had come to an abrupt end. Two other players, reserves who played, were also dropped from the squad for violating team rules. University president Kenneth Keller forfeited Minnesota's next game (January 26 at Northwestern), and shortly thereafter, coach Jim Dutcher resigned. I know Jim felt that he could not continue without the support of the university administration, but it was a sad way for an excellent coach, a highly ethical man and a valued friend to end his coaching years. Jim has maintained his ties to Gopher basketball as a broadcast analyst for Minnesota and other Big Ten games.

On January 30, the Gophers resumed their schedule, facing Ohio State at Williams Arena. Under interim coach Jimmy Williams, Minnesota, with three starters gone, was reduced to an "Iron Man" lineup. Joining previous starters, senior center John Shasky and senior guard Marc Wilson, were sophomore forward

Tim Hanson and two freshmen, forward Kelvin Smith and guard Ray Gaffney. Backed by some of the most enthusiastic crowd support I can remember, the Gophers upset the Buckeyes, 70-65. Shasky scored 19 points, and Gaffney showed what he would accomplish for the next three-plus seasons. Dave Holmgren played a minute and a half. He was the only Minnesota substitute.

The game did not erase the cloud of the seven days that preceded it, but the unwavering support of 13,443 fans certainly permitted a few rays of sunshine to beam through.

Who Was That Masked Man?

In 1989, the Gophers won their final three conference games to finish the regular season 17-11, and by the slimmest of margins, earn a berth in the NCAA tournament.

Minnesota was 14-2 at home but 3-9 away from Williams Arena. Because the NCAA games are played on a neutral court, not much was expected of the Gophers. To add to that, their leading scorer and second-leading rebounder, Willie Burton, suffered a broken nose in practice prior to the start of the tourney. Their number-one rebounder, Richard Coffey, was out with a knee injury.

With the guidance of trainer Roger Schipper and some finishing touches from Willie's mother, Burton was equipped with a face mask. It gave him the look of a "masked avenger," although it was white, making him the "good guy."

Good he was. I felt that the challenge of the mask made Willie a better player in the tournament games.

At Greensboro, North Carolina, Minnesota knocked off Kansas State, 86-75, as Burton racked up 29 points and 13 rebounds. Then the Gophers topped Siena, 80-67, with Burton contributing 19 points and 11 rebounds.

In the Sweet Sixteen at East Rutherford, New Jersey, Coffey came off the injured list to help with the rebounding, but Willie

Melvin Newbern lofts a pass to Masked Man Burton

again led the scoring with 26 points. It wasn't enough. Duke, led by Dan Ferry and Christian Laettner, eliminated Minnesota, 87-70.

Willie Burton averaged 17.9 points a game during the regular season. With the mask, he averaged 24.7 in the three NCAA games.

The Big Game

Ray Gaffney, a 6'2" guard from Dayton, Ohio, gave the Gophers four solid years from 1985 to 1989. He was the team's best three-point shooter and an excellent defensive player. He earned awards as Most Improved Player and Outstanding Student Athlete.

I enjoyed describing his four years on the court, but I remember most keenly a meeting at the Twin Cities airport in late

1989. I was returning from a trip; Gaffney was heading home to Dayton. He dug into his carry-on and pulled out his diploma. He was both proud and excited about it. You'd think he had just won the big game.

Which, of course, he had.

It's Sunday. Who's In Charge?

In March of 1990, I was in Richmond, Virginia, for the NCAA Regionals. On Friday, Minnesota had won an overtime game from Texas-El Paso and would play Northern Iowa late Sunday afternoon.

Saturday, in my hotel room, I got a call from a CBS television producer. He asked if I would tape an interview with Brent Musberger. Naturally, I said yes. When would it be?

He replied, "Twelve noon tomorrow."

I explained that I would be going to 11:00 mass, but that the church was nearby and I could get to the arena by no later than ten after 12.

His answer: "Nope. It's twelve noon or nothing."

I thanked him for considering me and told him it would have to be nothing.

In my pregame broadcast the next day, I reported the conversation exchange as diplomatically as I could and concluded, "I realize this is contrary to some opinions, but network television is not God."

In the week that followed, I got some of the most positive responses I've ever had.

The Best Single Half

I'm not sure which Minnesota basketball contest I'd rank as the best full game played by the Gophers. I do know which ranks on top as the best half.

In March of 1990, the Gophers finished 20-8, 11-7 in the Big Ten. That earned them a No. 6 seed and took them to the NCAA regionals at Richmond, Virginia.

The first game, with Texas-El Paso, was dreadful, but Minnesota overcame 33 percent shooting and struggled to a 64-61 overtime win.

The second game was as good as the first was bad, an 81-78 triumph over an excellent Northern Iowa team. Willie Burton had a career high 36 points and 12 rebounds.

The Sweet Sixteen, at New Orleans, was sweet indeed. Against favored Syracuse, Minnesota trailed 39-35 at the intermission. Now came my favorite half. In the second half, led by guards Melvin Newbern and Kevin Lynch, the Gophers shot 79.2 percent while holding the Orangemen to 37.1 percent. The final: Minnesota 82-Syracuse 75.

In the Elite Eight game, Dennis Scott of Georgia Tech kept hitting 3-pointers (he had seven threes and 40 points). Minnesota kept battling back. Burton, who scored 35 points, made a three with seven seconds left. 73-71 Georgia Tech. A quick foul, a missed Tech free throw, a rush downcourt, and Lynch's desperation three went off the rim.

I was disappointed, yes, but not crushed. This team had come far, and I had been privileged to share the ride.

Favorite "Away" Broadcast Locations

Please understand that I realize the need for the revenue generated by new stadiums and new arenas, but I miss the character, the "college spirit" of the stadiums and the fieldhouses/gymnasiums they have replaced.

Penn State's Bryce Jordan Center is an excellent facility, and the visiting broadcasters' location is spacious and comfortable, but my first Penn State-Minnesota broadcasts were from the top row of the old gymnasium (the top row was not all that far from the court), with students standing all the way around at the top. Penn State is a football school, but in the small confines of the gym, the percentage of students was high, and they supported their team enthusiastically. The new center seems sedate by contrast.

Michigan State's Breslin Center is also state-of-the-art, and, again, the broadcaster is well taken care of, but the Jennison Fieldhouse was, well, a fieldhouse. Our broadcast setup was located in the rafters but was uncrowded. What I remember most fondly is the system used to get the halftime and final statistics to us. Many decades ago, department stores used to enclose your money and the accompanying bill in a small container which was sent zinging on a wire cable to the lofty cashier's office. Shortly, your receipt and change would come zinging back down. As a boy, I thought it was the best of all transactions.

At Jennison, the stats crew worked at our height but on the opposite side. The crew would send the stats, enclosed in a small container, zinging across to us on a wire cable.

Jennison Fieldhouse was always noisy. So is Breslin Center. Michigan State really supports its basketball. But I miss the "zing."

From Just Short to All the Way

In 1993, the Gopher cagers finished the regular season 17-10. In the Big Ten, they were 9-9 but won 5 of their last 8 games. On the NCAA "bubble," they fell just short and were therefore headed to the National Invitation Tournament.

Minnesota was 14-2 on its home court, but Williams Arena began a major renovation immediately after the last regular season home game and was not available for any tournament games. However, the Target Center, home of the Timberwolves, could accommodate the first game, and if needed, a second game.

The fan turnout was huge. 11,944 fans saw the Gophers defeat Florida, 74-66. 18,254 cheered the victory over Oklahoma,

86-72. Learning that the Met Center was available (the home of the North Stars NHL team, which moved to Dallas the next season), the NIT decided on a third home game. Before 15,393 fans, Minnesota knocked off Southern California, 76-58, and headed for Madison Square Garden and the NIT's Final Four. (The three-game total attendance: 45,591.)

With a lot of Gopher supporters traveling to New York City, the Gophers overcame a second-half eleven-point deficit to beat Providence, 76-70.

In the title game, against Georgetown, Voshon Lenard was the only Gopher with more than one field goal in the first half. His 14 points were enough to give Minnesota a 32-30 lead. In the second half, Arriel McDonald was the only Gopher with more than one field goal. He scored 14 of his 20 points, Lenard had 17 for the game, and Chad Kolander blocked a final close-range Hoya shot, preserving a 62-61 championship win.

Lenard and McDonald were named to the NIT All-Tournament Team, with Voshon also earning the MVP honor. Minnesota finished the season 22-10.

Crittenden for Three

On February 16, 1994, the University of Minnesota Men's Athletics Department held a Hosea Crittenden Night.

Crittenden was a senior, listed at 5'9" (probably an inch shorter), from Rosemount, Minnesota. In his four years on the basketball team, Crittenden saw limited playing time but was a constant source of energy and inspiration to the entire squad. In home games where the Gophers had a huge lead with less than two minutes remaining, the "Crittenden" chant would begin, and Hosea would usually see action. As a sophomore, Crittenden sank a three-pointer, and he made a couple of two-pointers in later games, but in general, baskets were a rarity.

Now, it was Hosea Crittenden Night, and each fan, upon entering Williams Arena, was given a photo of Crittenden's face attached to a paddle. Late in the game, the Gophers led Penn State by a double-figure margin, and Crittenden, of course, did get to play. The crowd wanted him to shoot. A creature of habit, Hosea passed the ball instead. Finally, with less than a minute on the clock, he did shoot, and he was fouled. Two shots. Surely he would now score? Both throws clanked off to the side. His teammates once more got the ball to him with only a few seconds remaining. Hosea let the ball fly. A perfect three-pointer!

The crowd erupted with joy, and on the air, so did I.

The Triple O.T.

On March 5, 1994, Minnesota and Iowa met at Williams Arena. In special halftime ceremonies, Lou Hudson's jersey number, 14, was officially retired. As it turned out, the game itself was far from being half over.

At the end of regulation, the score was tied, 73-73. With Minnesota trailing by three points in the closing seconds of the first overtime, Voshon Lenard let fly a desperation shot. He drained it with four seconds left. 80-80. The second overtime produced more scoring but again ended in a tie, 92-92. The Gophers broke it open in the third O.T., outscoring the Hawkeyes 15 to 4 to win, 107-96.

I still retain the image of an exhausted Voshon Lenard, sprawled in the lane after the final horn. He had played 51 minutes out of 55 and scored a career high 38 points. (The year before, also at Williams Arena, Lenard scored 32 points in a 91-85 victory over Iowa.)

Arriel McDonald played 50 minutes and scored 22.

I broadcast three triple-overtime games in my forty-five years of Gopher basketball. Minnesota won all three, 70-68 at Butler in 1973, 57-55 at Iowa in 1982 and this win, also over Iowa. The Gophers went beyond three overtimes only once, a six-overtime 59-56 triumph at Purdue in 1955. That was two seasons before I started my Minnesota basketball play-by-play, but I well remember listening to it. All of it.

*An exhausted Voshon Lenard after the
triple overtime win over Iowa*

Jayson's Double Doubles

The Golden Gophers opened the 1994-95 basketball season with three late November games in Anchorage, "The Great Alaska Shootout." Anchorage is an attractive, modern city (non-Anchorage Alaskans regard the city as being "about thirty miles outside Alaska"), but I saw very little of it. The temperature did not rise above zero (Fahrenheit) until the day we left.

What I did see was Jayson Walton have three of the best games of his career.

In game one, the Gophers rallied from a 42-31 halftime deficit to defeat highly-regarded Arizona, 72-70. Walton scored 16 points and had 10 rebounds. Minnesota held Wildcat star Damon Stoudamire to 17 points on 5-for-15 shooting. The 15th shot was a three-point attempt that bounced off the rim as the game ended.

The next day, the maroon and gold topped Villanova, 85-64, as Walton had 14 points and 10 rebounds.

The title game was an excellent see-saw, with the Gophers beating Brigham Young, 79-74. Jayson Walton had his third straight double double, 11 points and 15 rebounds, and Minnesota took home the championship trophy.

Three Choices

I have broadcast Gopher tournament games in Hawaii, Alaska, New Jersey, California, Louisiana, Virginia, North Carolina, Missouri, Texas, Washington, New York, Oregon, Kentucky, Florida, Pennsylvania, Michigan, Illinois, Ohio, Connecticut, Alabama, Indiana and Puerto Rico.

The San Juan Shootout in Puerto Rico in November-December of 1996 is, in some ways, the most memorable. It was played in what could best be described as a small gymnasium. Gopher fans made up over half the spectators. In atmosphere, it was like a home game.

Our radio setup was marginal at best, but somehow we got on the air for all three games. The Puerto Rican team, Puerto Rico-Mayaguez, was Minnesota's first-round opponent. The team changed most of its players' numbers from those on the roster given us and on the printed program. The numbers even included some ending in six through nine (not permitted by the NCAA).

The Gophers won the tournament, but the concessions available to the fans remain my lasting memory.

The concession vendors offered a choice of three items:
1. Popcorn
2. Piña coladas, without rum
3. Piña coladas, with rum.

Seven in Eighteen

On January 8, 1997, at Assembly Hall in Bloomington, Indiana, the Golden Gophers trailed Bob Knight's Hoosiers, 79-72, with less than a minute to play. At the 52-second mark, Eric Harris hit a three-pointer. 79-75. Neil Reed of Indiana was fouled quickly, made both free throws, and it was 81-75. With 39.6 seconds left, Harris fed Sam Jacobson, who hit a three. 81-78. Time-out Minnesota. With 35 seconds remaining, Neil Reed's inbound pass was intercepted by Courtney James, who passed to Bobby Jackson, and he hit a three from the top of the key. 33.8 seconds left, and the game was tied, 81-81. In eighteen seconds of playing time, Minnesota had come from seven down to tie, the best sudden comeback I have ever described.

A few seconds later, Quincy Lewis blocked Andrae Patterson's layup, then missed a jumper himself as regulation time ended.

The overtime was less eventful. Jacobson hit an early driving layup. He added a short jumper almost a minute later, and at 2:38 of the 5-minute overtime, a 10-foot jumper. 87-81 Minnesota, and Indiana never got closer than four points.

Jacobson fouled out, but Lewis replaced him and hit two layups and a pair of free throws. Jackson added another three-pointer, and Minnesota had a 96-91 victory.

A remarkable finish for Minnesota, and a remarkable finish for Coach Knight. He appeared to remain calm throughout all of it.

My Favorite Basketball Pass

On February 26, 1997, at Crisler Arena, Minnesota had a chance to clinch the Big Ten title, but the Gophers trailed Michigan by four with two minutes left.

Minnesota got within two. Then Bobby Jackson tied the game with a baseline jumper from an "impossible" angle. Thirty-eight seconds to play, but the Wolverines were holding the ball near center court, letting the clock wind down for a last-second shot.

Suddenly, Eric Harris knocked the ball out of the hands of Louis Bullock. Harris dove for the ball, and while sliding on his stomach, batted the ball to Jackson, who drove to the basket and was fouled with 2.9 seconds remaining.

Bobby missed the first free throw but made the second. 55-54, and Minnesota had clinched the conference crown.

Midnight Madness

On March 8, 1997, the Gophers concluded their regular season with an unexpected 66-65 loss to Wisconsin at Madison. The victory enabled the Badgers to gain a spot in the NCAA tournament. For Minnesota, not much changed. It was the Big Ten champion, with a 16-2 record. It finished 27-3 overall, and, on March 9, the next day, it was named the #1 seed in the NCAA Midwest Regional.

At Kansas City, the Gophers led Stephen F. Austin at the half, 46-17, and went on to win, 101-55.

Two days later, Temple's matchup zone defense was shrugged aside, and Minnesota advanced to the Sweet Sixteen with a 76-57 triumph.

In San Antonio I called two of the best games I ever saw the Gophers play. In the first, Clemson and Minnesota went to overtime. Here the Gophers had to score the last six points to force a second overtime. Led by Bobby Jackson (a career-high 36 points) and Sam Jacobson (29 points, equaling his career high), Minnesota got eight of the first nine points in the second O. T. and won, 90-84.

Now came UCLA, a perennial national champion. Behind by ten early in the second half, Minnesota wore UCLA down and pulled away to win, 80-72, reaching the Final Four for the first time.*

Next on the immediate agenda: the charter night flight home. "Home" meant Williams Arena, where fans started to gather as early as 5:00. Our plane landed shortly after 11:00. The ensuing procession to the Barn consisted of a police car with its revolving dome light, then me in my car, then the team bus. We must have gone through a dozen red lights, and it was on television! (Going through red lights legally does wonders for your ego.)

When we arrived at Williams Arena, there were 15,000 fans inside and another 2,000 outside. The "outsiders" knew there was no more room inside, but they still wanted to savor these special moments. And they could hear the cheers, long and loud, that filled the next half hour. I was the MC for the "Welcome Home," and at center court, I was surrounded by the incredible pandemonium.

Quincy Lewis: "Final Four, here we come!"

Each fall, the Gopher basketball squad starts its season with "Midnight Madness," an introduction to the new season that begins at midnight on the first legal day of practice. The Willams Arena occasion is replete with music, cheers, dancing, food, an intra-squad game and, well, madness.

My Midnight Madness, though, will always be the midnight of March 22, 1997.

* The Gophers lost to Kentucky in the Final Four at Indianapolis, 78-69.

Tale of the Tape

How do you define "athletics trainer?" Is it "one who wraps athletes in miles upon miles of tape?"

If you like big numbers, that's a start, but let's go to the heart of the matter.

An athletics trainer recognizes degrees of injury, when to respond quickly, when to ease the pain slowly.

An athletics trainer knows that thresholds of pain vary greatly from one player to the next. He knows when to be sympathetic, when not to be overly sympathetic.

An athletics trainer is a part-time psychiatrist. Players who may not confide in anyone else, may well confide in him.

I have known many University of Minnesota trainers, among them Jim Marshall, Doug Locy and Brent Millikin, and many team doctors, among them Dr. Elizabeth Arendt, Dr. Pat Smith and Dr. Rich Feist. All of them have been unfailingly helpful professionally and genuine in their friendship.

The two trainers I have known the best are the late Lloyd "Snapper" Stein and Roger Schipper. "Snapper" is waiting for me in heaven, cribbage board ready, the cards already shuffled.

I have gotten to know Roger best. Shortly after he became the basketball trainer (in 1985), WCCO Radio obtained the exclusive rights to Gopher football and basketball. This meant I could now travel with the team to each road game. In football, you don't get to know players, coaches and trainers as well as in basketball. The numbers are too great. In basketball, an average of a dozen players and a similar number of coaches and other staff travel, making personal contact much easier. Sharing the airplane and bus rides, an occasional meal and the ambiance of the training room with Roger Schipper has been a highlight of my last sixteen years of basketball play-by-play.

Roger talks of communication being a key to the trainer's role. Taping an athlete is an important injury-preventive measure, but the setting for the taping lends itself to communication. This setting attracts not only players but the coaches as well. Schipper has a definite "don't take sides" attitude regarding players and coaches, but by listening to both, he can become an intermediary, if needed.

An athlete occasionally tries to play with pain, and the trainer's job is to make certain that excessive pride by the player does not make the injury worse. At the same time, Roger admires mental toughness, and cites Richard Coffey (1987-90), Chad Kolander (1992-95) and John-Blair Bickerstaff (2000-01) as excellent examples of that trait.

Schipper appreciates the camaraderie among the trainers of the Big Ten. If a Gopher player is injured on the road, and Roger needs to accompany him away from the court, perhaps away from the arena, a simple exchange of nods between trainers assures Schipper that the home school trainer will "take care of his guys" in his absence.

Trainer Roger Shipper attending J-B Bickerstaff

Big Ten game officials also have high praise for the treatment (physical and otherwise) they receive from trainers in the conference, something not always found elsewhere.

An athletics trainer may be the one who wraps athletes in miles upon miles of tape, but that's only the cover of the book. What's inside is the heart of any athletics program.

Out of the Depths

The 1997-98 basketball season had one of the most amazing final three weeks I have ever broadcast. After a 7-4 non-conference record, Minnesota went on to lose its first 6 Big Ten games. It then won 6 of the last 10 but was still 13-14 going into the Big Ten Tournament, the first year of that tournament. The Gophers would need to win 4 games in 4 days to qualify for the NCAA postseason. Very unlikely. They would need a .500 record or better to qualify for an NIT bid. Also unlikely.

They started out with a 64-56 win over Northwestern. Guard Eric Harris sealed the victory by making 7 of 8 free throws in the last minute of play. Minnesota was now 14 and 14, but its next opponent was top seed Michigan State. Minnesota had lost by 14 points and 12 points to the Spartans during the regular season. Another loss would end the Gopher season.

In one of Minnesota's finest upsets, the maroon and gold knocked off Michigan State, 76-73. Eric Harris played the greatest game of his career, with 29 points, 4 of 6 on three-pointers and 10 of 12 from the field overall. He held Mateen Cleaves to 13 points and just 2 for 18 from the field.

In the semifinals, the Gophers lost to Michigan, 85-69, but they were now 15-15 and eligible for the National Invitation Tournament.

The first three games were played at Williams Arena. Behind great crowd support, Minnesota beat Colorado State and Alabama-Birmingham handily, then won a thriller from Marquette, 73-71, on Sam Jacobson's reverse layup with 25 seconds to play.

On to Madison Square Garden for the NIT Final Four. In December, Minnesota had beaten Fresno State by 20. This game, however, was a nail-biter. Fresno State led 77-74 with 5 seconds left when Quincy Lewis, near the left corner, moved back a step to put him outside the 3-point arc, then sank a shot that sent the game into overtime. Kevin Clark, Lewis and Jacobson then led the way in a 91-89 overtime win. The same threesome took charge in the All-Big Ten final, and Minnesota defeated Penn State 79-72.

The Gophers, at one point 7-10 and 0-6 in conference play, wound up a 20-game winner and the NIT champion.

King of the Road

Every play-by-play man should have a Harry. For almost forty years, my road games were engineered by a variety of people, most of them skilled, a few of them less than skilled, each different from the other.

Then, for nine years, Harry McIntyre of Chicago was my technician/producer. I thought I knew a lot of people along the college circuit. Harry knew everybody. A technician is best measured by his handling of an emergency, and there are always emergencies. Harry handled them all with a cool disregard for broadcast air time, ticking ever closer. We always made it.

He was also a good mealtime conversationalist, at times quite philosophical. Harry at work was a "nuts and bolts" guy with a soft center he tried to mask.

Now, the "nuts and bolts" guy is writing very cerebral poetry, using words that say exactly the right thing but occasionally send me to the dictionary.

Harry, you will always be "Sovereign of the Thoroughfare." Naaah... "King of the Road."

Georgia on His Mind... Again

On December 28, 1999, at Stegeman Coliseum in Athens, Georgia, the Gophers trailed Georgia 65-64 with just a few seconds left. After an inbound pass, the play that had been planned was blocked by a defensive move. John-Blair Bickerstaff made a move of his own. With 3.1 seconds remaining, he scored on a lay-up, and Minnesota had a win on the road, 66-65.

On November 19, 2000, at Williams Arena, the Gophers trailed Georgia 74-73 with just a few seconds left. Again, J-B Bickerstaff made his move. With 11 seconds on the time clock, he sank another layup, and it was 75-74. Two added free throws eight seconds later made the final 77-74 Minnesota.

In that second game, senior Bickerstaff was 8 for 8 from the field for 17 points. Freshman Michael Bauer had 21. Both players later had their seasons cut short by in-game broken bones.

John-Blair Bickerstaff driving to the hoop

My Top Ten (Eleven) in Basketball

If the Big Ten can have eleven teams, my list of the top ten Gopher basketball players can also total eleven. This team dates back to the 1956-57 season when I began broadcasting Gopher basketball. My choices are all players I have described on the air during my career. The players I've chosen deserve it. Memory is fascinating, although unreliable. You may well have other deserving candidates. Maybe we can talk about it some day.

These are listed in the order they first lettered:

Ron Johnson (C-'58) Did everything well, very efficient

Ray Cronk (F-'60) Lean but strong, tireless, led the fast break

Lou Hudson (F-'64) My all-time favorite, the complete player

Jim Brewer (F-'71) Amazing inside player, my favorite rebounder

Flip Saunders (G-'74) Floor leader, top free thrower, destined to be a coach

Mychal Thompson (C-'75) The smoothest, most fluid Gopher

Ray Williams (G-'76) My favorite guard, did so many things well

Kevin McHale (F-'77) A young colt, all knees and elbows but a force

Trent Tucker (G-'79) All-around player, shot threes before they were in the rules

Willie Burton (F-'87) Outstanding in college, erratic in the pros

Bobby Jackson (G-'96) Average stats, all he did was win games

*Former Gopher teammates Mychal Thompson
and Kevin McHale tangle in the NBA*

Louie

Louis (Louie) Brewster lettered in Gopher basketball in the 1940s. His first letter came in 1943. Then, like several of his teammates, he served in the military in World War II before returning to campus and lettering in 1946 and '47. A starting guard all three seasons under Dave MacMillan, Brewster specialized in the long set shot and setting up his teammates. These included Tony Jaros, Don Carlson, Bud Grant (all played later with the Minneapolis Lakers) and, for Louie's senior year, Jim McIntyre, who twice earned All-American honors.

After graduation, Brewster became a successful businessman on local, national and international levels, but he never forgot his University of Minnesota roots.

Each year, the basketball alumni play in an alumni-versus-alumni game, adjacent to a varsity game. I don't remember Louie ever missing one of these games. His teammates always saw to it that he took several of his long set shots, and he usually sank one or two.

The key word with Louie Brewster is "support." He often wrote letters of encouragement to the coaches and others closely involved with the basketball program, including me.

The most complete demonstration of that support came on cold winter nights when the Gopher charter airplane would arrive, well after midnight, taxiing to a point some distance from any warm shelter. There, at the foot of the plane's steps, stood Louie. Occasionally, he might miss an arrival if the Gophers had won. He never missed if they had lost. He knew when he was needed most.

Louie Brewster died during the 2000-2001 season. A week or so later, I remember descending the charter plane's steps, well after midnight on a cold winter's night.

Louie was not visible, but I knew he was there.

The Computer Age

Computers have increased the speed with which statistics are made available during the play-by-play of football and basketball games.

Computers also generate tons of information for the pages given the media as preparation for a game.

For a Gopher preconference game in the 2000-2001 basketball season, this invaluable data was included in the pregame handout at Tallahassee. I present it in its entirety:

"Florida State is undefeated (1-0) when it outscores its opponent this season."

An Unexpected Recognition

On February 28, 2001, I was courtside at Assembly Hall in Bloomington, Indiana, over halfway through my pregame broadcast, preceding the Minnesota-Indiana game. We paused for the National Anthem. It came in very clearly. My engineer/producer Marc Gurstel had told me he had a direct line to the PA system. This was unusual, but I didn't question it.

I had just resumed my pregame commentary when I became aware that Don Fischer, Indiana's football and basketball play-by-play man for many years, and Kit Klingelhoffer, Indiana's associate athletics director, were standing directly in front of me. Marc managed to shut me up (in mid-sentence), and Don Fischer, on the PA and on our Golden Gopher Basketball Network, paid tribute to my fifty years of Gopher football and forty-five of basketball broadcasts. Kit then presented me with a plaque, containing a piece of the old Fieldhouse basketball floor and a piece of the original Assembly Hall basketball floor. I had broadcast Minnesota-Indiana games at both locations. When Don finished, the Indiana fans not only applauded but stood up and applauded.

I realize I am not a household name in Bloomington, much less Indiana, but Indiana fans respect tradition, especially basketball tradition, as much as any fans anywhere. And yes, I've been around so long that I am tradition.

I had trouble getting back on the air coherently. I have always found Indiana fans to be knowledgeable and supportive of their team, and now I have an extra bond with them.

The Barn

Williams Arena began in 1928 when it was built at a cost of $650,000 and named the University of Minnesota Fieldhouse. In its early years, it also housed indoor track and field facilities, tennis courts and other sports, including winter football practices.

In 1950, it was remodeled, the floor became permanent, and the arena was named after Dr. Henry L. Williams, a longtime early Gopher football coach.

I don't know when the affectionate term "The Barn" began, but it was there when I started broadcasting Gopher basketball in the 1956-57 season. Extensive remodeling in 1992 and again in 1997 transformed the lower-level locker room, training room, etc., improved the comfort level of the seating and streamlined the overall appearance, inside and out.

However, Williams Arena remains eternally "The Barn." The basketball floor itself is elevated three feet. I keep waiting for a serious player accident to happen. It hasn't, and most fans and players like the raised floor more than I do.

A personal note. Players always come charging onto court, up the steps from the lower level. They often comment on the surge of adrenaline when they hit the top step and hear the roar of the crowd. This was never completely real to me until I was honored at halftime of my final regular season Gopher broadcast March 4, 2001.

I waited, halfway up those steps the players use. Then, as I was introduced, I climbed the remaining steps, hit that magic top step and heard the roar of the crowd. It took me 45 years of broadcasting, but now Williams Arena, "The Barn," has become part of me, deep inside. As a spectator, I stand and cheer the Gopher players as they come into view, and I know how they feel. I was there. Just once. It lasts a lifetime.

A Sad Ending... a Promising Beginning

In 1999, the University of Minnesota ended its regular season 17-9, 8-8 in the Big Ten. It lost a close game to Illinois in the opening round of the conference tournament, 67-64, but was still chosen for the NCAA playoffs. Its first-round game was scheduled for March 11 in Seattle against lower-seeded opponent Gonzaga.

The morning of the game, the "scandal" broke. Four Gopher players were named as having class papers written for them by an athletics department academic counselor. The four were dropped from that night's roster, and Minnesota lost to Gonzaga, 75-63.

Gonzaga, extremely well-coached by Dan Monson, was a fiercely competitive team, and continued on to the Elite Eight.

The repercussions of the scandal included the forced resignation of Minnesota coach Clem Haskins, players leaving the program, a variety of self-imposed and NCAA sanctions, and the hiring of a new coaching staff, with Monson named as head coach. One of Monson's most recent games was the tournament victory over Minnesota. Now he was in charge of reviving the stricken Gopher program.

I spent my final two broadcasting years with Dan, his staff and his players. They were two very good years, a truly satisfying way to end my career.

Dan Monson still has a couple of NCAA hurdles left. None were of his making, but he has grabbed the challenges willingly, and Gopher basketball is becoming Golden again.

The Big Ten Title

The majority of Big Ten sports decide the conference champion in what is usually a three-day tournament at the end of the regular season. In football and basketball, the champion is determined by what happened in eight conference football games and in sixteen conference basketball games. Please understand that I have always enjoyed broadcasting tournaments and NCAA and NIT postseason playoff games. Also understand that I remember, nostalgically, how important it once was to win the Big Ten championship in football and basketball. Now, those titles too often seem to be simple stepping stones to what follows the regular season.

In football, a 6-5 record usually means a postseason berth, and the better the record, the more prestigious the bowl game. In basketball, try to finish in the top five, because that means a bye in the first round of the Big Ten tournament, and 20 wins is often the magic number for an NCAA selection.

I recognize the added exposure, the added revenue, the added player incentive of the postseason games, but I'd still like a little more tingle of excitement in striving to capture the Big Ten title. Not the Something-dot-com Bowl, not the conference tournament final, not the Final Four... but the Big Ten Title. Make that the initial goal, and then let's go on from there.

Out of Circulation—Into Tradition

These are the numbers retired by the University of Minnesota's Men's Athletics Department and the players who made the numbers immediately recognizable:

Football	72	Bronko Nagurski	(1927-1929)
	54	Bruce Smith	(1939-1941)
	10	Paul Giel	(1951-1953)
	15	Sandy Stephens	(1959-1961)

Hockey	8	John Mayasich	(1952-1955)

Basketball	14	Lou Hudson	(1964-1966)
	52	Jim Brewer	(1971-1973)
	43	Mychal Thompson	(1975-1978)
	44	Kevin McHale	(1977-1980)

Editor's Note: List reflects numbers as of the first publication of this book in 2002.

Wrestling

Wrestling With World Hunger

Norman Borlaug was born near Cresco, Iowa, in 1914. His home was on a small grain and livestock farm. His elementary school was a one-room, one-teacher schoolhouse. After graduation from Cresco High School, he entered the University of Minnesota. There, he earned a bachelor's degree in forestry in 1937, a master's degree in forest pathology in 1941 and a Ph.D. in plant pathology and genetics in 1942. From 1935 to 1937, he also earned three letters as a Gopher wrestler.

Leaving the university, Norman Borlaug then turned to his most challenging opponent: world hunger.

Working in the fields with the same stamina and competitive spirit he displayed as a Gopher wrestler, he tried and rejected methods and ideas until he found the right ones. The wheat fields of Mexico, especially, were his laboratories. Within twenty years, he found a disease-resistant wheat, short-strawed and high in yield.

He worked to put new varieties of wheat, corn and rice into major production to feed the hungry people of the world. Wheat strains developed by Norman Borlaug, harvested first in Mexico, India and Pakistan, can now be found in Latin America, the Middle East, the Near East and Africa.

In 1970, Borlaug was awarded the Nobel Peace Prize for his "Green Revolution."

Borlaug's International Wheat Improvement Program has trained thousands of young scientists from many different countries. Their work in production and nutrition has expanded around the globe.

Norman Borlaug has received recognition from countries and universities worldwide. One of the most satisfying came in 1968 when the people of Ciudad Obregon, Sonora, Mexico, where he did much of his early work, named a street in his honor.

That street has no end. It is a humanitarian avenue that crosses all boundaries.

The Brothers Z

There have been several brother combinations on University of Minnesota athletics teams, but if you're listing them in alphabetical order, make sure you go all the way to the bottom of the list to find two of the top performers: the Zilverberg brothers, Larry and Dan, from Hopkins, Minnesota.

Larry wrestled from 1974 to 1976, winning Big Ten titles at 158 pounds in 1974 and '75 and at 167 pounds in 1976. He earned NCAA All-American honors all three years.

Dan also wrestled for coach Wally Johnson. He lettered from 1978 to 1980, winning Big Ten titles at 158 pounds in 1979 and '80 and NCAA All-American both years.*

Their career records: Larry   82-4-1

Dan   119-11-2

Dan's final two years were remarkable, 45-3 each year.

* Vern Gagne was Minnesota's only four-time Big Ten champion, winning the heavyweight crown in 1944, '47 and '49 and the 191-pound title in 1948. Gagne also won the NCAA 191-pound title in 1948 and the heavyweight crown in 1949. Gagne, for many years an outstanding professional wrestler, is a consistent supporter of the Gopher wrestling program and of Minnesota athletics in general.

Mentor Morgan

Marty Morgan is J Robinson's head assistant. No one could serve as a better example to varsity veterans and incoming recruits alike.

Morgan, a graduate of Bloomington, Minnesota's Kennedy High School, won an NCAA Division II national title in 1988 as a freshman at North Dakota State.

He transferred to the University of Minnesota and went on to become a three-time NCAA All-American, and as a senior, an NCAA Division I 177-pound champion. In his junior year, he pinned twenty-one opponents, a school record that still stands.* As a senior in 1990-91, he went 39-0 and won the Big Ten Medal of Honor.

Marty continued to wrestle after graduation, winning two Greco-Roman national titles and placing twice in the National Freestyles. In the 1992 Olympic trials, he finished third at 198 pounds. In the '96 trials, wrestling at 180 pounds, he finished second.

Two of Marty's brothers also had Olympic competition— John in 1988 in Seoul, South Korea, and Gordy in 1996 in Atlanta. Gordy was the Big Ten 158-pound champion for the Gophers in 1989.

In 1999, Marty Morgan, a member of the University of Minnesota Men's Athletics Hall of Fame and the Minnesota Wrestling Coaches Association Hall of Fame, was named the National Wrestling Coaches Association Assistant Coach of the Year.

* Billy Pierce holds the school career pins record with 51 pins between 1992 and 1996.

Another 39-0

At Durand, Wisconsin, Tim Hartung won the state title once, wrestling at 152 pounds. He came to the University of Minnesota with high hopes but no high predictions. Hartung worked on technique, strength and bulk. He grew to 197 pounds and went on to establish credentials similar to those of his coach, Marty Morgan. In 1998-99, Hartung matched Morgan's season record of 39-0 (the only two Gophers wrestlers to post unbeaten records. The year before, Hartung went 39-1). Tim's 39-0 was part of a winning streak of 58 matches, a U of M record.

Like Morgan, Hartung capped his senior year by winning the Conference Medal of Honor.

Tim Hartung became the first Minnesota wrestler since Vern Gagne (1948 and '49) to win consecutive NCAA titles, the 190-pound in 1998 and the 197-pound in '99.

He won three Big Ten crowns in 1997, '98 and '99 and was named Big Ten Wrestler of the Year in 1999. In November and December of 1997, he scored falls in eight straight matches. (Marty Morgan is second in that category, with six.)

In four years, Tim Hartung added about forty pounds and a whole lot more.

Tim Hartung in another of his 58 straight wins

The First Four-Timer

Chad Kraft won three state titles while at Lake-Okabena-Lakefield High School. He brought with him a strong belief in the wrestling coaches and their program and in the University of Minnesota.

In 1996, as a freshman wrestling at 150 pounds, he finished fifth in the NCAA championships, earning All-American honors. A third place, then a second place, the following two years garnered two more All-Americas. Since 1936, there had been many Gopher All-Americans, some of them three-time winners. No four-time.

In 1999, now wrestling at 157 pounds, Chad Kraft placed fifth and became the first Gopher four-time All-American. Through his four years, Chad increasingly became the focus of recruits who realized, "If he can do it, maybe I can be a four-timer too." Chad Kraft has brought in high school graduates who share his belief that a University of Minnesota wrestler can indeed be a medal winner from the very beginning. Head coach J Robinson emphasizes how important Kraft's achievement has been to the entire program. Entering the 2001-2002 season, Minnesota had six wrestlers with a chance at being All-American four times: Luke Becker, Damion Hahn, Jared Lawrence, Garrett Lowney, Leroy Vega and Jacob Volkmann.

Lesnar and Oklahoma State

In January of 2000, Minnesota and Oklahoma State met twice in a span of thirteen days. Both events were decided in the final match.

January 9, the fourth-ranked Gophers took on third-ranked Oklahoma State at Stillwater, Oklahoma, where the Cowboys had won seventy-three consecutive matches over a four-year stretch.

After nine of the ten matches, there had been no pins and only one major decision, Brandon Eggum of the Gophers at 184 pounds. Oklahoma State, with five wins, led 15-13 going into the heavyweight final.

Brock Lesnar came through with a pin at 3:48, giving Minnesota six points and a 19-15 triumph, ending Oklahoma State's long home victory string.

January 22, the two teams met in the semifinals of the Cliff Keen/NWCA Duals Tournament at University Park, Pennsylvania.

The rankings were now reversed. Minnesota was third, Oklahoma State was fourth

Again there were no pins, and this time, not even one major decision through the first nine matches. With a 5-4 edge in decisions, the Cowboys led, 15-12.

Once more, Brock Lesnar made the difference. Scoring the only major decision of the event, Lesnar earned four points, giving the Golden Gophers a 16-15 victory.

The next day, Lesnar almost did it again. Minnesota trailed Second ranked Iowa State, 17-12, after nine matches. Lesnar scored a major decision-four points-but couldn't quite manage a six-point pin. The Gophers lost, 17-16, ending a 23-dual match win streak.

Try, Try Again

Leroy Vega of Portage, Indiana, has more than established himself as an important ingredient in the University of Minnesota wrestling program.

An All-American each of his first three years, Vega is pointing toward making that four in a row.

The Gophers' unparalleled comeback to win the NCAA title in 2001 is one of his greatest thrills, but for sheer tenacity, how about the match with Iowa's Jody Stritmatter, February 18 of 2001 before 10,048 fans at Carver-Hawkeye Arena. Iowa had won fifteen consecutive home duals, and, more important, Stritmatter had defeated Vega in all five of their previous encounters.

At 125 pounds, the two battled on even terms through regulation, with each earning four extremely hard-fought points. In the overtime, Vega scored a takedown to come away with a 6-4 win, his first in six matches again Stritmatter.

The decision proved to be of crucial importance. By a 17-16 score, Minnesota ended Iowa's winning string, finished 8-0 in Big Ten dual meets, won the Big Ten title again, and less than a month later at the same Carver-Hawkeye Arena, gained its first NCAA championship.

Leroy Vega and Coach Robinson poised for action

"Ten - Ten - Ten"

"Ten" is the main word in one of the greatest team efforts ever, giving the University of Minnesota the 2001 NCAA Wrestling Championship.

During the season, the Gophers lost only one dual meet, to Oklahoma State. They won the next fourteen duals, finishing 19-1 overall and 8-0 in Big Ten competition.

At the Big Ten championships, sophomore Jared Lawrence, at 149 pounds, and freshman heavyweight Garrett Lowney took individual titles to spearhead a 24-point team triumph. All ten Minnesota wrestlers placed in the top seven, meaning all ten qualified for the NCAA tournament.

At Iowa City on March 15, the Gopher NCAA beginnings were very disappointing. Not one Minnesota wrestler qualified for a title match, meaning no first or second place points. It also meant an extraordinary effort was needed in the third through eighth place matches. A team championship was a slim hope, at best.*

On March 16th and 17th, the team gave its response. All ten U of M matmen finished in the top eight, giving Minnesota enough points for the NCAA crown and giving all ten All-American status.

Wrestling at Carver-Hawkeye Arena, the home of so many championship Iowa teams, the Gophers had accomplished the nearly impossible. Small wonder coach J Robinson, his staff and his team led the Gopher fans at the arena in a resounding chant of "Ten - Ten - Ten!"

Luke Becker, Owen Elzen, Chad Erickson, Damion Hahn, Brett Lawrence, Jared Lawrence, Garrett Lowney, Brad Pike, Leroy Vega, Jacob Volkmann.

Ten.

*Coach J Robinson, who never gave up hope, was chosen Coach of the Year by the National Wrestling Coaches Association.

The 2001 NCAA Wrestling Champions

Two in a Row

In March of 2002, the Gophers repeated as NCAA team wrestling champions. It wasn't a dramatic comeback this time, and it wasn't at Iowa City, but at Albany, New York, Minnesota finished 23.5 points ahead of second place Iowa State, and for the first time ever, the Gophers had two individual champions, Jared Lawrence at 149 pounds and Luke Becker at 157.

Becker's win was especially satisfying. Luke had lost to top seed Bryan Snyder of Nebraska in five of their previous six matches, including a double-overtime 5-4 loss earlier in the season. This match also ended 5-4 in double-overtime, but this time Becker had the 5.

Only three Minnesota wrestlers finished higher than their NCAA seed, but champions Lawrence and Becker return next year as seniors, and those non-seniors who finished below their seed and certainly below their expectations have added incentive for next year.

A three-peat? Could be.

Early Start

Many of Garrett Lowney's achievements came before his first All-American. After compiling a 155-5 high school record (including 97 pins) at Freedom, Wisconsin, Lowney was 10-2 as a Minnesota freshman in 1998-99.

Given an extra redshirt year to train for the Olympics, he captured a gold medal at the 20-and-under Greco-Roman World Championships, then took a third at the Pan-American Championships. In June of 2000, Lowney qualified for the Olympic Games by winning the 213-pound Greco-Roman title at the Olympic trials.

At Sydney, Australia, Garrett, the youngest member of the American wrestling team, scored four victories over seasoned veterans in the 213-pound Greco-Roman class to earn an Olympic bronze medal. Only two other Gophers had ever done this: Jim Martinez, a bronze in 1984, and Brandon Paulson, a silver in 1996.

Returning to the University, Garrett Lowney won the Big Ten heavyweight title in 2001, went 22-1 overall and placed third for an All-American in the NCAA Championships.

There's a lot more to come!

Tension on the bench: J Robinson, Marty Morgan, Eli Ross

J

J Robinson's first fifteen years at Minnesota have been a powerful success story. Coming to the university after nine years at Iowa (the last year as interim head coach), Robinson saw his first squad go 7-14 overall, without winning a single Big Ten dual meet. The turn-around came quickly. In the second season, the Gophers were 15-6, and from then on, J's only losing season was '91-'92 when the 8-14 mark reflected the difficult decision to redshirt two outstanding wrestlers to keep a balance among sophomores, juniors and seniors in the immediate season to come.

As Minnesota's wrestling program's prestige grew, so did recruiting success. Incoming freshmen were learning that they too could make an immediate impact.

J Robinson's overall winning average is 72.8 percent overall and 64.1 percent in Big Ten duals. In the last five seasons, the Gophers have been 89 percent overall and 90 percent in the Big Ten.

With several Big Ten Coach of the Year awards, J Robinson has now coached an NCAA champion at Minnesota and is the 2001 National Wrestling Coaches Association Coach of the Year.

The Answer

Around 1970, I represented University of Minnesota sports at a fathers and sons all-sports dinner at Temple Israel in Minneapolis. Representing professional wrestling was Leonard "Butch" Levy, who had won the 1941 NCAA heavyweight championship as a Gopher wrestler and had gone on to fame as a pro wrestler and promoter.*

During the question-and-answer session, a boy about ten years old, raised his hand, was acknowledged, then asked Butch:

"Mr. Levy, is professional wrestling a fake?"

My personal feeling was and is that pro wrestling is an entertainment. College wrestling is a sport. I wondered how Butch could answer the ten-year old truthfully but without disillusioning the boy.

Butch Levy looked down at the questioner and gave one of the best answers I have ever heard.

"Young man," said Levy, "everything you see in that ring is really happening."

* Levy also lettered in football from 1939 to 1941 and in baseball in 1942

Hockey

"Maroosh"

John Mariucci was an outstanding end, playing both ways, for Bernie Bierman's 1937-38-39 football teams. Defensively, his crushing tackles made him feared throughout the Big Ten. As a Gopher hockey defenseman, his crushing body checks inspired the same fear.

In 1940, All-American Mariucci was the key to Minnesota's undefeated season and the AAU National Championship.

Following his stellar Gopher career, "Maroosh," from Eveleth, Minnesota, went on to play NHL hockey for five years with the Chicago Blackhawks. On a Canadian-dominated team, he was the "enforcer." Mariucci's fight with Black Jack Stewart of the Detroit Red Wings is still regarded as the longest battle in National Hockey League history. It lasted over half an hour.

In 1952, Mariucci accepted the head coaching job at the University of Minnesota. He took a team that had gone 13-13 the year before all the way to the NCAA title game, finishing with a 22-5 record and earning him Coach of the Year honors.

Mariucci may have played pro hockey on a mostly Canadian team, but at Minnesota, he sought homegrown talent, only rarely going outside state boundaries.

"Maroosh" spurred the development of amateur hockey at every level in Minnesota. While he became known as the "Godfather of American hockey," partly because of his combative history with the Blackhawks, he truly raised the state of Minnesota to the pinnacle of amateur hockey nationwide. It is fitting that the University's magnificent hockey arena bears his name.

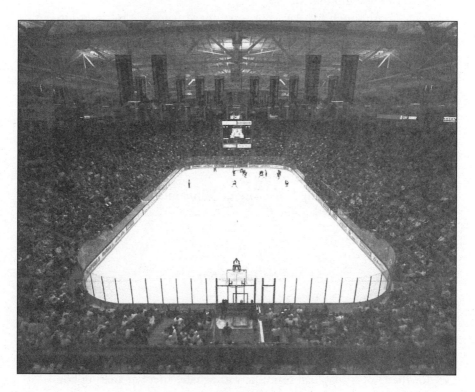

Mariucci Arena

An Eveleth Encore

In John Mariucci's first year as Gopher head coach, 1952-53, another Eveleth, Minnesota native, John Mayasich, helped his coach and his school rocket to national prominence. "Rocket" is also the word used for Mayasich's slap shot. He was the first college player to develop that weapon.

Although his slap shot was indeed fearsome to opposing players, Mayasich was basically a finesse skater, incredibly talented on blades. When the Gophers were a man short because of a penalty, it's said that Mayasich would kill the entire penalty time without ever passing the puck. Under other circumstances, he was an expert passer. In his Minnesota career, he averaged almost one and a half goals and almost three points a game.

A multiple All-American, John Mayasich still holds Gopher career records for points (298) and goals (144) and single game records for goals (6) and points (8).

He is the only University of Minnesota hockey player to have his number (#8) retired.

The Hot Spot

From 1956 to 1958, Jack McCartan stopped a lot of hard shots. As goalie for the Gopher hockey team, the Saint Paul, Minnesota native had a career save percentage of 90.8. As third baseman for the U of M baseball team, he was equally adept at snaring hot drives.

In baseball, McCartan's best year at bat was 1956 when he hit .436 with a .779 slugging percentage (and these were pre-aluminum-bat days). Jack was All Big Ten all three of his years and All-American in 1958. With McCartan at third base, Minnesota won the NCAA title in 1958 and the Big Ten championship in '58 and '60.

Two Iron Range legends: John Mariucci and John Mayasich

In the nets for the hockey Gophers, McCartan had a career goals-against average of 2.95. (In both 1956 and 1957, his GAA was 2.80). In 1958, he was named a hockey All-American and was awarded the Big Ten Conference Medal of Honor.

The climax to his career came two years later when he was the goaltender for the United States gold medal hockey team in the 1960 Olympics.

The Referee

Glen Sonmor coached Gopher hockey from 1966 to 1971. I don't know if this poem is his creation, but he's the one I heard recite it:

> I think that I shall never see
> A satisfactory referee,
> One who calls them as they are
> And not as I would have by far,
> A gent who bends not either way
> But lets the kids decide the play.
> Poems are made by fools like me,
> But only God can referee.

Mighty Mite

Mike Polich was one of the smallest players in Minnesota when he starred for Hibbing High School. Glen Sonmor recruited him anyhow. The results proved Sonmor to be a shrewd judge of talent.

By the time he reached the University of Minnesota, Polich had grown to a height of 5'8". Under coach Herb Brooks, Polich led the Gophers in scoring his last three years (1972-73 through 74-75). The Minnesota center scored a four-year total of 159 points in 148 games (32, 52 and 62 points the final three seasons).

Playing on the Gophers' 1974 national championship squad, Mike was named to the NCAA All-Tournament team. In 1975, he became an All-American, was co-MVP in the WCHA and Gopher MVP. He also won the Big Ten Conference Medal in 1975.

Polich went on to star in the National Hockey League. He was a member of the Montreal Canadiens Stanley Cup Champions in 1977 and played for the Minnesota North Stars from 1978 to 1981.

Polich says he always looked forward to an opponent featuring big players. Mike says he could outskate them. Against a smaller-sized team, his job was tougher. What about now? Polich says all the big men can skate now. The little guy no longer has the advantage.

Maybe not now, but in the 1970s, Mike Polich used that advantage to the fullest.

The Prelude to "Miracle On Ice"

While Herb Brooks is best known nationally and internationally for coaching the United States team to victory in the 1980 Olympics (that team had twelve Minnesota players on its roster), he had already established a championship mode at the University of Minnesota.

Brooks coached for seven years at Minnesota, winning three NCAA titles, with one second-place finish.

The first crown came in Brooks's second year of coaching, 1974. After an 0-4-1 start, the Gophers went 8-0-1 in the next nine games. Eventually, with a 17-11-5 record, they won the WCHA playoffs, defeating Michigan twice, tying, then beating Denver. In the NCAA finals at Boston, Minnesota, led by goalie Brad Shelstad and centers Mike Polich and John Harris, edged Boston University, 5-4, then dominated Michigan Tech, 4-2, for the title (it was 4-1 until the final minute).

Two years later, in the WCHA playoffs, the Gophers took two from Colorado College. Then at East Lansing, the U of M tied Michigan State, 2-2, before winning an epic triple-overtime 7-6 match from the Spartans. In that game, Gopher goalie Jeff Tscherne had 72 saves, a team mark that still stands. The 1976 NCAA finals, at Denver, were a repeat of the 1974 opponents, and the outcomes were the same. Minnesota beat Boston, 4-2, and Michigan Tech, 6-4. In the title game, the Gophers overcame a first period deficit of 3-1 to win. Tom Vanelli had a goal and four assists, earning tournament MVP honors. Minnesota finished the season 27-13-2.

The final NCAA championship came in Herb Brooks's final year, 1979. First came a four-game sweep of the WCHA playoffs, Michigan Tech twice and Minnesota-Duluth twice. In the NCAA finals at Detroit, the Gophers edged New Hampshire, 4-3, then topped North Dakota by the same score. Minnesota finished 21-11-1, winning ten of the last eleven games.

Herb Brooks' 62.4 percent winning record at Minnesota was exceeded later by Brad Buetow (69.0 percent) and Doug Woog (66.4 percent), but until 2002, no one else captured an NCAA crown, much less three of them.

Herb Brooks in his Gopher years

The Hobey Baker Award

Hobey Baker was an outstanding and inspirational hockey player at Princeton almost a century ago. It is said that before every game, he visited the opponents' locker room and shook hands with every opposing team member. Baker epitomized the word sportsmanship and was an outstanding player, too.

The award bearing his name was established in 1981, honoring one player each year who showed the same exemplary qualities on and off the ice that made Baker a legend that lived on after he lost his life as a World War I pilot.

University of Minnesota center Neal Broten of Roseau, Minnesota, was honored as the first recipient of the Hobey Baker Award. Broten played for the Gophers in 1979-80, then for the 1980 Olympic champion US team, returning to Minnesota for the 1980-81 season. Neal and his brother Aaron were teammates on the 80-81 squad, and Neal felt Aaron should have gotten the award. Both had the necessary credentials.*

In 1988, Gopher Robb Stauber of Duluth, Minnesota, became the first and only goalie to receive the Hobey Baker Award. Stauber was first team All-American and first team WCHA, with a 2.72 goals-against average.

The third U of M player to receive the award was center Brian Bonin of White Bear Lake, Minnesota in 1996. (Bonin almost received it in the previous year). During Bonin's four years, 1992-1996, Minnesota made two NCAA Final Four appearances and won three WCHA Playoff titles. He once scored at least one goal in twenty consecutive games.

Neal Broten, Robb Stauber and Brian Bonin have brought distinction to their home state and university through the Hobey Baker Award.

* Neal Broten is the only hockey player to win an NCAA title (1979), an Olympic Gold Medal (1980), the Hobey Baker Award (1981) and the Stanley Cup (with the New Jersey Devils in 1995). He is enshrined in the U.S. Hockey Hall of Fame.

*Minnesota's Three Hobey Baker winners:
Neal Broten-Brian Bonin-Robb Stauber*

"Darting"

Doug Woog worked his way through "speed, exciting, explosive, dashing," then settled on "darting" to describe center Corey Millen.

Woog first coached Millen in the 1982 World Juniors Tournament. Although Woog was not yet the head coach at Minnesota, he knew Millen had an outstanding future. When Woog took over the Gopher program in 1985, Millen, a Brad Buetow recruit, was already in place. He had missed playing for Cloquet in the Minnesota State High School Tournament because of a broken ankle, but he missed very little after that. Three NCAA tournaments (Millen was named to the NCAA All-Tournament team in 1987), the 1984 Olympic team, the team point leader two of his three Gopher seasons, then professional hockey in Europe and the National Hockey League.

One final note: in December of 1986, the Gophers won the Jeep/Nissan Classic in Anchorage, Alaska. Steve MacSwain and Corey Millen were front-line teammates on that squad. In Anchorage, Steve introduced Corey to his sister, Kelly. The meeting led to matrimony.

MacSwain got an assist.

Corey Millen facing off

Putting the "O" into "D"

Perhaps it's significant that Mr. and Mrs. Richards named their son Todd. The name has two D's and an O in it. Todd Richards, a solid defenseman from Robbinsdale, Minnesota's Armstrong High School, was also the top offensive defenseman of the mid '80s.

Doug Woog felt blessed in having Richards on his Minnesota squad from 1985 to 1989, Woog's first four years as head coach. Woog had a 74 percent-plus winning average those years, and he calls Todd his point guard (as in basketball). Richards distributed passes like a center or forward. As a defenseman, he had a career total of 128 assists, a team record, and 158 career points, one ahead of Mike Crowley. Todd's 128 assists are fifth on the Gopher career list, and the four players ahead of him are all forwards or centers.

Two D's and an O—that's Todd Richards.

The Drifter

Goaltender Robb Stauber of Duluth, Minnesota, could have gone to UMD (University of Minnesota Duluth). Superior, Wisconsin is Duluth's twin port, and the University of Wisconsin was interested, but Robb and his family had a passion for the maroon and gold, and those were the colors he wore with pride from 1986 to 1989.

After a 13-5 record as a freshman goalie, Stauber came into his own as a sophomore. He started all 44 Gopher games, had a goals-against average of 2.72 and a 91.3 percent saves average. He stopped an average of 38.9 shots a game and had 5 shutouts. As a sophomore, he was named first team All-American and became the first goaltender to win the coveted Hobey Baker Award.

Stauber's third and final Gopher season was equally impressive: a 26-8 record, a 2.43 goals-against average and a 91.1 percent saves average. He led Minnesota to its second straight WCHA title and to its third straight NCAA Final Four.

So why does his coach Doug Woog call him "the drifter?" Robb did not stay in the net. He could even be found in the corner, making passes. The best goalie puck-handler in the nation, he was credited with several assists.* Woog remembers him crossing his own blue line on occasion. It worked for Stauber. High school goalies, trying to copy his wandering style, discovered they were not nearly as agile as Robb.

Stauber retired as a player after a ten-year National Hockey League career, but he's still a volunteer goalie instructor for the Gophers. The maroon and gold passion continues.

* Stauber almost scored a goal against Michigan Tech. With a last-minute open net for Tech, Stauber fired an accurate shot toward the other end. Only a desperate midair swat by a defenseman kept Robb from a goalie goal.

The Corner Lot Rink

In White Bear Lake, Minnesota, the Bonin family had a corner lot with room for an ice rink in the winter, complete with shin-high boards. It was the gathering place for son Brian and the other hockey youth of the neighborhood. Sure, it was outdoors, but the parents didn't have to drive to an indoor arena for an extremely early morning ice time.

The transition to high school rinks (indoors) was smooth for Brian Bonin, as smooth as his skating. Coming straight out of high school (no junior hockey) to the University of Minnesota was tougher. Bonin's great instincts were always there, but body maturity would take a while.

Brian scored 10 goals as a freshman in 1992-93, then jumped to 24 as a sophomore, 32 as a junior and 34 his senior year. His assists rose each year, too: 18, 20, 31 and 47. His final year, he led the nation in scoring, was a first team All-American, was named WCHA Player of the Year, and in 1996, won the Hobey Baker Award.*

And it all began on an ice rink on a corner lot in White Bear Lake.

* For additional information on Brian Bonin, see "The Hobey Baker Award."

The Playmaker

When his coach Doug Woog talks about Mike Crowley, he uses terms like "positive attitude, love for the game, team player," but he settles on "playmaker" as the most apt. Crowley had an innate ability to "see" a play and go on from there.

From his high school days at Bloomington, Minnesota's Jefferson to his three Gopher seasons to his National Hockey League career, Crowley is remembered above all for his finesse as a puck-handler. The best way to kill off an opposing power play is to control the puck, and Mike has always done just that.

He was also a defenseman who scored. A first team All-American, he shared with Tony Kellin the team career record for goals by a defenseman—37. In January 2002, Jordan Leopold broke the record. In career points by a defenseman, Crowley has 157, one behind Todd Richards. In single season assists by a defenseman, he is both first and second: 47 points in 1996-97, 46 in 95-96. In career points by a defenseman, he again is the one-two leader, with 63 and 56.

He also was completely team-oriented. Woog says the only "I" in Crowley was in his first name.

Golden Goalie

February 18 and 19, 2000, the Gophers trounced Michigan Tech on the road, 9-2 and 4-1. Sophomore Adam Hauser was his usual solid self in goal, stopping 50 of 53 shots in the two games.

Shortly thereafter, it was discovered that Hauser had mononucleosis. While recovering, he missed the next four games, the final games of the regular season. Minnesota lost all four but did qualify for the WCHA playoffs.

March 10 and 11, Hauser returned to play Colorado College, and Gopher first-year coach Don Lucia faced many of the players he coached just a year earlier.*

The maroon and gold won the opener, 4-2. It was a one-goal game until an open-net score in the closing seconds. Hauser stopped 26 of 28 shots, and one of the Tiger goals came on a power play.

In game two, Colorado College led 2-1 until, with 8.8 seconds remaining, Erik Westrum tied the score. Stuart Senden's overtime goal gave Minnesota a 3-2 win. In the nets, Adam had 28 saves on 30 shots, and again one of the goals was on a power play.

For the season, Hauser had a record of 20-14-2.

The next year, as a junior, Hauser was 26-12-2 and was WCHA Player of the Week three times.

Although taken by Edmonton in the third round of the 1999 NHL entry draft, Adam Hauser chose to return to the Gophers for his final year.

* Lucia calls this series and the Gophers' return to the WHCA Final Five the high points of his first two seasons at Minnesota.

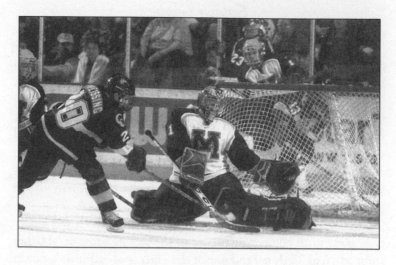

Adam Hauser with a save against Colorado College

Penalty-Killing

In the 2000-2001 season, the University of Minnesota hockey team set a school record for successful penalty-killing, with a percentage of .885. During a sixteen-game stretch in January and February, the Gophers stifled 86 of 89 opposing power plays, a mark of .966.

Senior Aaron Miskovich of Grand Rapids, Minnesota added three more short-handed goals during the season, giving him a career total of ten, tying the team record set by Paul Broten in the mid-eighties.

Coach Don Lucia's philosophy on penalty-killing is to be aggressive, but he also recognizes that it requires a strong goal-tender. He had one in Adam Hauser.

How about the Gophers' success when they had the power play advantage? Lucia says it couldn't have been accomplished without an outstanding group of freshmen. One of them, Grant Potulny of Grand Forks, North Dakota (Lucia's first non-Minnesota recruit) was expected to play a supporting role in his first season. Instead, he skated to the forefront, leading the nation with sixteen power-play goals. In addition, junior John Pohl of Red Wing, Minnesota, was second in the nation with thirteen.

A Standout Blueliner

As a freshman, Jordan Leopold of Golden Valley, Minnesota was the Gophers' Rookie of the Year, made the WCHA All-Rookie Team and was selected by Anaheim in the second round of the NHL entry draft.

As a sophomore, Leopold was named to the all-WCHA second team.

The best was yet to come.

As a junior, in the 2000-2001 season, Jordan tied with Travis Roche of North Dakota as the nation's leaders in the season's scoring by a defenseman. Both had 49 points, with Leopold playing in two fewer games. Leopold also became Minnesota's first All-American since Mike Crowley was named in both 1996 and 1997.

Leopold, who was a finalist for the Hobey Baker Award, could have turned pro with Anaheim but elected to stay with the Gophers for his senior season.

On Sunday, January 6, 2002, Leopold scored two third-period goals to defeat North Dakota, 2-1. The goals made him Minnesota's all-time leading scorer.

From Alaska to Colorado to Minnesota

As a youngster in Grand Rapids, Minnesota, Don Lucia was a radio rooter for the Gophers.* Once each year, Don and his father made the trip from northern Minnesota to Memorial Stadium to see a Minnesota football game. Lucia remembers, as a

Grand Rapids high school hockey player, being thrilled when the Gopher hockey team rallied to beat Michigan Tech, 6-4, to win the NCAA title in 1976. Best of all, two members of that championship team, Bill Baker and Don Madson, were from Grand Rapids. Lucia hoped that he would be the next Gopher recruit from his city.

A university recruiting visit actually was scheduled, then called off when the last opening was filled by someone else. Don wound up at Notre Dame and figured that his University of Minnesota dream would never come true.

After six years coaching at Alaska-Fairbanks and six more at Colorado College (with a winning percentage of .634 for the twelve years), Don Lucia got the call from Minnesota in April of 1999 and was quick to accept.

Despite his Minnesota background and his lifelong appreciation for Gopher hockey, Don says that, only now, being on the inside looking out, does he fully realize how complete the U of M fan support is. As he travels the state, Lucia finds the key word for that support is "passion," and he is passing that passion on to his players.

* I have had countless listeners say they heard my Gopher football broadcasts while raking leaves, washing windows, plowing fields or even hunting pheasants, but Don Lucia is the first to tell me that he and his dad listened while grouse hunting.

Hold the Presses!

In the preface, I stated that this book covers only events through the year 2001.

Then came March of 2002 and the Gopher wrestling championship. Next came April of 2002 and the Gopher NCAA hockey championships. The publisher was very accommodating, and both events were fitted into the book.

The wrestling title repeat is described in "Two in a Row."

The hockey title was anything but a repeat. The last University of Minnesota hockey crown came in 1979.

The 2002 Frozen Four was played in Saint Paul. Gopher coach Don Lucia appreciated the home crowd advantage, but would it be enough?

On Thursday, April 4, Minnesota edged Michigan in the semifinal, 3-2. Grant Potulny of Grand Forks, North Dakota, the only non-Minnesotan on the team, scored twice.

The Gophers built a 3-0 lead, then held on to win despite two Wolverine goals late in the third period.

On Friday, April 5, U of M defenseman Jordan Leopold became the fourth Gopher player to win the Hobey Baker Award (see "The Hobey Baker Award"). Leopold's 20 goals this season made him the highest-scoring defenseman in college hockey. For the season, Leopold had 20 goals and 28 assists. In his four-year career, he totaled 45 goals and 99 assists.

Then, Saturday, April 6, Minnesota vs. Maine for the title. A strong third period gave Maine a 3-2 lead. With one minute to play, Minnesota trailed, and the clock was ticking seconds and tenths of seconds. Then, Matt Koalska scored with 53 seconds remaining, and the game went into overtime.

How do you rally tired legs for one more all-out effort? Coach Lucia decided, in his words, "a change in undergarments" might freshen his squad in more ways than one.

Whatever the inspiration, the Gophers out-played Maine in the overtime, and on the only power play of the O.T., Grant Potulny again became the hero, shoving the puck home for the first Minnesota NCAA crown in twenty-three years.

The two wins in the Frozen Four gave goalie Adam Hauser a career total of 83 victories, setting a WCHA record. Hauser had 42 saves in the championship game.

And, this *very* last minute "Hold the Presses." On June 1, 2002, the Gopher men's golf team, faced with budget-cutting extinction only two months earlier, won its first-ever NCAA Championship, shooting a 6-under par the final day to beat second-place Georgia Tech by four strokes. Minnesota, the first northern team to win the national crown since 1979, had trailed Tech by three strokes going into the closing round.

Golf

Harris and Nielsen - Opposite Approaches

John Harris lettered in golf from 1971 to 1974 and in hockey the same four years. Jeff Nielsen lettered in hockey from 1991 to 1994 and in golf in 93 and 94. The two had the same pairing of sports, but there the similarity ended.

Harris was the "Master Thinker." In golf, he plotted each course, each hole, each stroke. In hockey, under split-second circumstances, he still seemed to sense the pattern of a play even before the play took form.

Nielsen was a "natural" at golf. He stepped up to the ball, decided how hard he needed to hit with the club he had in hand, took aim and swung. Hockey too was an instinctive approach for Jeff.

Harris was a golf All-American in 1973 and 74, All Big Ten in 1973 and the Big Ten champion in 1974. He continues to be a Walker Cup player and won the U.S. Amateur championship in 1993.

Since graduating, Nielsen has been a National Hockey League player, but don't challenge him to a golf match, or, if you do, don't play for money.*

* Since this was first written, a shoulder injury ended Jeff Nielsen's hockey career. Jeff's next goals: successful rehab for the shoulder, then a successful try at the pro golf tour.

Slap Shot with a 5-Iron?

Former Gopher hockey coach Doug Woog loves to play golf. He's not a scratch golfer, but a lot of former Gopher hockey players are—among them, John Harris, Jeff Nielsen, Neal Broten and Robb Stauber. Woog and Stauber even conduct a combined hockey-and-golf summer camp.

Are hockey and golf that compatible? Woog says they are, without a doubt.

The hand-eye coordination are similar. You break your wrists on a golf shot and a hockey shot. Your hips follow through on both. You pass or shoot to a specific spot in hockey, just as you have a specific target in golf. The two sports have similar motor skills.

Finally, Woog says hockey players literally take thousands upon thousands of swings at the puck, and that's good preparation for the golf swing.

So keep your eye on the puck, keep your eye on the ball, and good luck.

"Birdie Day"

In 1998, the Gopher golf team qualified for the NCAA championships for the sixth straight year. The first round at Albuquerque, New Mexico, was a near disaster. Of the 30 teams competing, Minnesota stood 29th. Since only the low 15 teams would make the cut after round two, it appeared that Minnesota was hopelessly out of it.

The team had an afternoon tee time for the second round. Many of the morning scores were low, which made the team feel even worse. Coach John Means took an opposite approach. He told his five players: "Look at those scores. This is a birdie day. Go out there and make some birdies!"

1998 NCAA Champion James McLean

The number 5 man, Bill Thompson, sank a 30-foot putt for a birdie. Number 4 Adam Dooley followed with a 15-foot birdie putt. The "Birdie Day" had begun.

Team standings were posted every three holes. Here's what the Gophers saw that day:

After 3 holes - 29th place
6 holes - 26th
9 holes - 22nd
12 holes - 17th
15 holes - 15th
18 holes - 12th

Minnesota had made the cut (eliminating host school New Mexico, which dropped to 16th), shooting the lowest NCAA tournament round ever, 16 under par.

The maroon and gold went on to finish 7th and enabled Gopher James McLean to win the individual title with a 271 score. Had the U of M missed the cut, McLean would have played only two rounds — no individual crown. The "Birdie Day" changed all that.

The Best Ball-Striker

Former Gopher golf coach John Means regards Martin LeMesurier as the best ball-striker he has ever seen. LeMesurier, an import from England, who played from 1997 to 2000 and was a three-time All-American, had an uncanny accuracy in his drives and second shots. According to Means, a bucket could be placed well out in the fairway, and often as not, LeMesurier would plop his shot into the bucket.

With the team practicing in its indoor facility, the Goodrich Golf Dome, Means took a recruit over to watch LeMesurier. The coach pointed to one of the 3-inch-wide air holes, 70 yards away, in the ceiling of the Dome.

"See how close you can come to that air hole, Martin."
LeMesurier took three shots with his 4-iron. All three balls
disappeared into the air hole.

Northern Golf

Former Minnesota coach John Means realizes Minnesota
winters move golf to indoor facilities, but he says that can help, not
harm. Means is one of golf's best teachers, and he feels he can
teach best when no one is keeping score. Fundamentals are a top
priority for Means, and working and teaching indoors helps focus
the player on his stance, grip, swing and more.

John admits that recruiting below the Mason-Dixon Line
was tough, but, in addition to corraling the talent from Minnesota
and the Upper Midwest, he established a close rapport with coaches
from foreign countries. That, plus Means's success as teacher and
coach, brought recruits to the university from Australia, England,
Sweden, Canada and other distant locations.

Means and track coach Phil Lundin had a friendly rivalry
over which team would have the better academic record. Over the
past four years, the golf team has averaged better than a 3.0.

"Yes Sir, Mr. Bolstad"

When John Means was a high school senior at Burnsville,
Minnesota, he competed in the State High School Golf Tournament at University Golf Course (which has become the Les Bolstad
Golf Course). This was 1973, and in those days, the tourney's 36
holes were played in one day.

Means was taking some early-morning practice swings when
he saw the legendary Bolstad approaching. Bolstad had already
completed twenty-seven of his thirty years as Gopher coach and
was truly an icon in golf.

Tom Lehman with an earlier hairstyle

Thinking, "He likes my swing, he wants to correct my swing, he's going to ask me to come to Minnesota" and similar thoughts, Means tried to appear nonchalant as Bolstad reached his side.

The coach put his hand on Means' shoulder.

"Hi. I'm Les Bolstad."

"Oh, yes sir, Mr. Bolstad. I know who you are."

"It's going to be a long day out there. You might want to take along a sandwich."

Tom Lehman

In the summer of 1978, former Gopher golfer Rick Ehrmanntrout played in the Resorters Tournament at Alexandria, Minnesota. A local golfer caught his eye. He told the Gopher staff it should go after this guy. The staff did, and Rick's eye proved to be accurate beyond measure. Tom Lehman, who had planned to attend St. John's University at Collegeville, Minnesota, wound up in the maroon and gold.

Lehman became the school's first three-time All-American, lettering from 1978 to 1981. He was All Big Ten in '79, '80 and '81.

Former Gopher coach John Means believes in the three Ds for success at the college level—Desire, Discipline and Dedication. While Means did not coach Lehman, he feels Lehman epitomizes all three of the Ds, with special emphasis on dedication. Means knows of no golfer with a greater dedication to the game than Lehman.

Tom Lehman excels on and off the pro tour, serving the game of golf and serving his state and nation through his considerable charitable efforts.

Baseball

Two-Sport Standouts

Paul Giel and Dave Winfield both were high-profile baseball players for Dick Siebert. Both went on to have careers in major league baseball. Both were key players in one other Gopher sport.

Paul Giel of Winona, Minnesota, was first team All-American and first team All-Big Ten all three of his years (1952-1954). He still holds the school record with 243 career strikeouts. His career earned run average was 2.16. In 1952, he fashioned an ERA of 0.42.

Paul is usually remembered even more for his football exploits. Passing, running, punting, returning punts and kicks and playing defensive back, Giel was twice All-American, twice Big Ten Most Valuable Player, Associated Press Back of the Year and United Press International Player of the Year.

He rushed for over 100 yards in nine different games (nine-game seasons then) and set what were then school records for rushing and passing yardage. His football jersey number, #10, has been retired.

Dave Winfield, of Saint Paul, Minnesota, was All-Big Ten three times as a pitcher (1971-1973), with a 19 and 4 record, an All American in 1973. He had an earned run average of 1.48 in 1971. His 109 strikeouts in 1973 is one behind Mike Diebolt's record of 110. In his three years, Dave fanned 229.

When he wasn't pitching, Winfield played in the outfield. He had a career batting average of .353.

Winfield also played two years of Gopher basketball, for the 1971-72 Big Ten champions and the 72-73 second place squad. His averages reflect his improvement:

	FG	FT	REB	PTS
71-72	.484	.654	5.4	6.9
72-73	.512	.704	6.1	10.5

Paul Giel is enshrined in the College Football Hall of Fame.

Dave Winfield is enshrined in the Major League Baseball Hall of Fame.

Dave Winfield celebrating a 1973 home run against Purdue

Three Extra-Inning Games in Omaha

The University of Minnesota baseball team, under Dick Siebert, took the national championship at Omaha in 1956, 1960 and 1964.

In 1956, Jerry Thomas was the pitching star. Thomas beat Arizona twice, 3-1 and 12-1.* Shortstop Jerry Kindall later coached three Arizona teams to national titles, becoming the only man to both play for and coach a national champion.

In 1964, the Gophers got only one hit in a 4-1 loss to Missouri, but came back to beat the Tigers in the deciding game 5-1, behind Joe Pollack's four-hitter. Pollack got the win in three of the four Minnesota victories.

Midway between the 1956 and 1964 crowns came the memorable 1960 College World Series, with three great games between the Gophers and Southern California. Both teams were 2-0 in the double-elimination tournament, going into their first confrontation. Trailing 11-2 in the seventh inning, Minnesota rallied to force extra innings, then won it in the 10th, 12-11.

After each team beat a different opponent, they met again. The Trojans needed a victory to force a final game. They got it, an 11-inning 4-3 squeaker.

The next day, the two teams again went into overtime. This time, a bases-loaded walk gave Minnesota a 2-1, 10-inning triumph and the NCAA title.

Gopher second baseman John Erickson was named the tournament MVP.

* In 1956, Thomas pitched 121 2/3 innings, still a school record.

"Molly"

Paul Molitor's introduction to head coach Dick Siebert came in the late summer of 1974. John Anderson was sitting in

Siebert's office when Molitor, an incoming freshman, stuck his head in the door, intending just to say hello. "Molly" then had a beard and a long, flowing hairdo. "The Chief" looked up, peered at the intruder, then said "Who the heck are you?" (or words to that effect).

"I'm Paul Molitor."

"Well, Molitor, before our first practice tomorrow, shave off that beard and get a haircut."

Molitor did.

He also went on to be first team All-American in 1976 and '77. His batting achievements came with bats made of wood. Most Big Ten hitting records have come in the last few years, in the age of aluminum bats, but Molitor could do it all. At Cretin High School in Saint Paul, at the university and in the major leagues, he played the game with an effortless grace that tended to obscure his intensity and his awareness of every potential situation.

One of his very first games with the Gophers showed what was to come for the next two decades-plus.

"Molly"

Playing against a very good University of Texas team at Austin, Texas, Molitor got on base his first at-bat. Advancing to third base, he looked at the left-handed pitcher, then whispered to third base coach George Thomas, "I think I can steal it," nodding toward home plate. "Okay?"

Thomas thought it over, then gave him the go-ahead.

Molitor did steal home, then trotted to the dugout. Siebert, whose eyesight was diminishing as his health declined, looked up from his ever-present scorecard.

"What happened? Did you get picked off?"

"No, Coach, I stole home."

"Who told you you could do that?"

"I checked with Coach Thomas."

"Okay. If you get another chance, do it again."

In the same game, Molly got another chance and did it again.

The Little Guy Wanted to Be Here

Brian Raabe had two things going for him when he first came to John Anderson's office in 1986. He was from New Ulm, Minnesota, with its resounding baseball legacy (most recently, the Steinbachs, Terry and Tom, had played for the Gophers in the early eighties), and he had a relentless determination. Nonetheless, he was small, his arm was questionable, and the Gopher coaches had three second base candidates ranked ahead of him.

Raabe declared, "No disrespect to those guys, but I'm gonna beat 'em out. I want to be here."

To "be here," he worked constantly on every phase of his game. To gain arm strength, he threw a football over and over.

Perhaps the best example of his character came in an early-season game at the Metrodome. Pitcher Denny Neagle had a 1-0 lead in the sixth inning, opposing runners on second and third, with two outs. The batter hit a grounder right at Raabe. Right through his legs. Two runs scored.*

When the inning ended, Raabe went directly to Anderson.

"Coach, if you'll ever play me again, I'll never do that again."
He did play again. He played a lot. He made the plays.

In 1990, he was a first team All-American and was drafted by the Minnesota Twins.

* The Gophers did rally to win that game.

Dan Wilson awaits the throw

Pitch It or Catch It?

As a Gopher and as a Seattle Mariner, Dan Wilson has always been a team player. Coaches Anderson and Fornasiere put him at the top of the list of "best people."

Wilson came to Minnesota from Barrington, Illinois, and incidentally, helped bring future Illinois recruits to Minnesota. His first year, he was both a pitcher and a catcher, 6 and 1 as a pitcher and equally impressive as a catcher.

John Anderson and Wilson sat down at the end of the 1988 season. Anderson felt Wilson should concentrate on one position. Dan felt he could do more for the team in a dual role. Wilson had been named Big Ten Player of the Year as a catcher, and they finally agreed that one position, catcher, was the best solution, both for the team and for Wilson's future career.

Wilson used his strong arm to throw out base runners, handled pitchers well, was a solid hitter and always a humble, selfless contributor to the maroon and gold cause.

A first-round draft pick by Seattle in 1991, his approach to the game and his team remains unchanged.

Sorry, Dad

In the spring of 1987, Rob Fornasiere, longtime Gopher assistant head baseball coach, was returning from a recruiting trip. Although Minnesota had already recruited and signed a shortstop, Fornasiere stopped in Grand Rapids, Michigan, to watch a high school shortstop from Grandville, Michigan. Rob was impressed, made some notes but no offer.

That fall, two weeks into practice, the recruited-and-signed shortstop blew out his knee. The Gopher staff got on the phone to Grandville and the home of Brent Gates. Brent's father wanted his son to stay in the state, sign with Michigan or Michigan State, but Brent agreed to make a visit to Minnesota.

The timing couldn't have been better. The Twins were in the World Series. Gates had come alone on his visit. He and his Gopher host were able to buy tickets on the street and saw a Series game in the Metrodome. Gates was very impressed with Minnesota, the Gopher staff and players and the university's baseball tradition.

Gates returned to Grandville, cancelled his other visits, and still to his father's dismay, signed with Minnesota.

The Gopher coaches converted Brent to a switch-hitter.

With a tennis background, he felt that his backhand made the left-handed addition easy. Gates was a natural hitter. John Anderson says Gates never worried about what a pitcher was throwing. "He saw the ball, and he hit it." He batted in the number-two spot in his first game as a Gopher. He did well. Anderson moved him to number three for the second game, and there he stayed for the rest of his U of M career.

An extremely consistent hitter, Gates had a career batting average of .387, hitting .412 in 1991, earning Big Ten Player of the Year honors.

The Plan

When Rob Fornasiere visited Minnetonka, Minnesota High School pitcher Jim Brower on a 1991 recruiting visit, the 18-year old Brower told him not to worry. He was coming to Minnesota, and he had a Plan.

1. For now, he would turn down all major league offers.
2. He would pitch for the Gophers for three years.
3. He would then be drafted and pitch in the major leagues.

Brower did reject all offers and did pitch for three years for John Anderson. Although he was the Gopher Pitcher of the Year in 1994, his college career was good but not great. However, true to the Plan, he was drafted (in the sixth round) by the Texas Rangers, was traded to Cleveland, then to Cincinnati.

Once he made it to the majors, he seemed to relax and become a better and better pitcher.

Jim Brower's "Plan" is complete.

Merila's Biggest Victory

In 1991, Mark Merila of Robbinsdale, Minnesota's Armstrong High School played second base for the Gophers and was named Big Ten Freshman of the Year. In 1994, as a senior, he was Big Ten Player of the Year.

In between, he was a first team All-American his final two years and made the change to a switch-hitter successfully. It took a while, but, in 1993, he batted .408 and in '94 set a team season mark of .452. Merila's career average of .393 is a school record, and his keen eye, plus his threat at the plate, led to 187 career walks, another Gopher high mark.

Mark Merila's greatest victory lay ahead. Late in his senior year, he suffered seizures. A brain tumor was discovered. Although radiation treatments to shrink the tumor could have dangerous side effects, Merila elected to go ahead with radiation. The treatments were successful.

Merila was taken into the San Diego farm system where he was given the choice: continue playing in the minors or join the Padres as a bullpen catcher. He chose the bullpen, and John Anderson feels he will wind up as a coach in the majors some time soon.

Easy to Recruit

John Anderson says Robb Quinlan may have been his easiest recruiting job. Quinlan, of Maplewood, Minnesota and Hill-Murray High School, didn't need convincing. His older brother Tom had almost come to the University of Minnesota, then signed instead with the Toronto Bluejays.

Robb, "always a Gopher," came to the U in 1996, and in his four years, established school career records in eight hitting categories. He set Big Ten career marks in hits (345), runs (249), doubles (79) and home runs (55). His career batting average was .381, slugging average .677.

The Big Ten Player of the Year in 1999 at first base, Quinlan also played the outfield. Coach Anderson says Robb was an outstanding defensive first baseman and, at the plate, had a bat speed comparable to that of Paul Molitor.

Almost as fast as he first signed to play for the Gophers.*

* Robb Quinlan was drafted in 1999 by the Anaheim Angels.

The Pregame Ceremony

When Kerry Ligtenberg came out of Park Cottage Grove, Minnesota High School, he was 6'2" but a skinny 150 pounds. Nonetheless, he could pitch, and the Gophers welcomed him aboard.

Ligtenberg added 35 pounds and 10 miles per hour on his fastball, but there were no major league offers. In the late spring of 1994, former Gopher and Atlanta Brave Greg Olson offered Kerry a chance to pitch for his Minnesota Loons team. It was summertime employment, so Kerry accepted the opportunity and did well. As a scout, Olson recommended Ligtenberg to the Braves. The Braves made an offer. Kerry needed one more class, three credits, to get his chemical engineering degree. The class was held only in the spring, half a year away. John Anderson felt he should take the Braves' offer, and Ligtenberg agreed.

Pitching for the Atlanta Double-A farm team, Ligtenberg got noticed and was brought up to the parent club. He stayed.

The story isn't over. Janet Piercy is as avid a Braves fan as you will find. Her husband George, an Exxon executive, was a Minnesota graduate, who contributed generously to the university. When the Piercys learned of Braves pitcher and former Gopher Ligtenberg being three credits short of his degree, they went to work. Janet Piercy made innumerable phone calls to Professor Frank Bates at the University, pleading Kerry's case. It helped that he had been a good student.. When the University switched from the quarter system to semesters, Bates was able to retabulate Kerry's credits. He had more than enough.

In the summer of 2000, on the field, just before a Braves home game, Professor Bates presented Kerry Ligtenberg with his chemical engineering degree. Janet Piercy led the applause.

Ligtenberg, a closer on the Atlanta pitching staff, had brought his three-credit quest to a close.

Battling Back

On May 1, 2001, the baseball Gophers were struggling again. In preseason, pitcher Dan McGrath lost his appeal for one more season of eligibility. On March 3, pitcher Ben Birk took a line drive to the face, sustaining multiple fractures. Without two of its aces, the team went 9 and 10 in the first month and a half. John Anderson had never had a losing season. Nor would he in 2001. The team rallied magnificently, winning 20 of the next 25. Then came a setback. In late April, at Columbus, Ohio State swept four games from the Gophers.

Two nonconference games got them back in the win column. The next Big Ten games were with Northwestern May 11-13 at Siebert Field. Minnesota took all four games, eliminating the Wildcats from the conference playoffs. Ben Birk, in his first action since the injury, pitched three courageous innings. Third baseman Jack Hannahan provided his usual solid at-bats and made a tumbling-into-the-seats catch of a foul popup to end the final game when Northwestern had the tying and go-ahead runs on base.

Minnesota now moved into the Big Ten tournament at Columbus, where the Gophers had lost four straight one month earlier. The tournament was double elimination, but the maroon and gold never reached a do-or-die game.

Minnesota defeated Penn State, 4-2. Next came a 15-11 win over Illinois, in which Jack Hannahan celebrated his being named Big Ten Player of the Year* by going 4 for 5 with two home runs and seven runs batted in. (The RBI total tied a tournament record set by Gopher Jeff Monson in 1991.) Game three was against

Ohio State. Minnesota won it, 6-5. Finally, in game four, Ben Birk added proof to his comeback, going seven innings for the victory in a 3-2 win over Michigan.

Minnesota, with ten straight wins, eight in the Big Ten, had earned an automatic bid to the NCAA Tournament.

The ten-game string and the season ended in the regional at Baton Rouge, but it was a rewarding ride.

* Hannahan led the Big Ten in hits, runs, home runs, total bases and slugging percentage (.766). His .402 batting average was second in the league.

Celebrating the 1998 Big Ten baseball title

How to Follow a Tough Act to Follow

Dick Siebert coached University of Minnesota baseball from 1948 to 1978. During that span, he had 754 victories. His overall winning percentage was 67.6, in Big Ten games, 66.0 percent. "The Chief" earned his nickname, establishing a program that was the envy of college coaches everywhere.

John Anderson came to Minnesota after a year at Hibbing Junior College (not far from John's northern Minnesota high school, Nashwauk-Keewatin). As a walk-on, he was impressed with the level of talent and wondered if he could make the grade as a pitcher. A shoulder injury answered that question, and he then wondered if he should transfer to a smaller school where he still might be able to compete effectively. Anderson had just taken Dick Siebert's coaching class, achieving the highest score ever given by the Chief. Siebert suggested that he stay on as a student assistant.

With Siebert's failing health forcing more duties onto Anderson, the newcomer coach worked very closely with the team in the 1977 season. It turned out so well that when the team took an end-of-the-season vote to determine the most valuable player, John Anderson's name led all the others. Siebert felt that a full-time player, not an assistant coach, should be named MVP. He insisted on another ballot. This time the vote was unanimous: John Anderson. Siebert gave in.

Dick Siebert's poor health ended his career (Siebert died in December of 1978), and his chief assistant, George Thomas, took over. He chose Anderson as his right-hand man.

Three years later, Thomas resigned, and, in the fall of 1981, Anderson, at age 26, became the youngest head baseball coach in the history of the Big Ten.

How do you live up to your mentor's legendary achievements? You do your best to continue to expand the Siebert program and make it your own. Anderson has done just that.

From 1982 through 2001, he surpassed Siebert's Big Ten victory total with 312. At the end of the 2001 season, his 728 career wins were just 26 behind the Chief.

Dick Siebert (1948-1978)

John Anderson (1981-)

Siebert and Anderson, over 50 years
of coaching Gopher Baseball

Other 20-year marks:

5 Big Ten titles (4 as Big Ten West champion, one as Big Ten champion. The conference discontinued the East-West divisions in 1988)

7 Big Ten tournaments

7 Big Ten tournament championships

12 NCAA postseason appearances,

Twice Big Ten Coach of the Year

In October of 2001, John received the Dick Siebert Award, given by the Minnesota High School Baseball Coaches Association to a person who has done much to promote high school baseball.

John Anderson has already proven himself to be a tough act to follow.

Tennis

Noyce and Geatz

The resurgence of the Gopher men's tennis program began in the fifteen-year tenure of head coach Jerry Noyce. In Noyce's final ten years, Minnesota never finished below third place in the Big Ten, sharing the conference crown in 1981 and winning it outright in 1984 and '86.*

The Gophers had finished second in the Big Ten in 1987 and '88 when David Geatz took over in 1989. Geatz wasted no time. His U of M team went 21 and 9 and captured the conference title. From 1992 through 1995, the maroon and gold was unbeaten in 45 consecutive Big Ten matches, winning the conference championship all four seasons. Over those four years, Geatz's teams won 94 while losing 17, a winning percentage of .847.

In Geatz's first thirteen years, Minnesota has had a .679 winning percentage, making the NCAA regionals eight straight times and reaching the round of sixteen three of those times. Geatz has been named Big Ten Coach of the Year three times (1991, '92 and '94) and NCAA Region Four Coach of the Year twice (1994 and 2000).

David Geatz feels even better rewards lie ahead for the Golden Gophers.

*As a Gopher student-athlete, Jerry was All-Big Ten in 1964, '65 and '66 and team MVP all three years.

Tennis coach Dave Geatz

From Novosibirsk to 4.0

Find a globe. Put a finger of one hand on the Twin Cities of Minneapolis-Saint Paul. Put a finger of the other hand on Novosibirsk, Siberia. You'll need both hands because the cities are on opposite sides of the globe. Unless you fly the Arctic Circle route, they're half a world apart.

An American businessman who owns restaurants in Siberia got word to Gopher coach David Geatz that he had discovered a skinny kid in Novosibirsk who could really play tennis. Investigation proved it to be a genuinely good lead, and Alex Zharinov made the long trip to Minnesota.

Now came the tough part. The University of Minnesota requires all international students to pass the Toefl Test, an English proficiency examination, to gain admission.

Zharinov spoke very little English. Although he worked very hard at mastering the language, the summer of 2000 found him failing the Toefl Test three times. His fourth and final try came the day before fall semester began. A fourth failure would mean a return to the other side of the globe.

He passed by three points.

Alex Zharinov became the Gophers' number-4 singles player, was in strong contention for Big Ten Freshman of the Year and had a grade point average of 4.0.

Alex Zharinov, from Novosibirsk

The Minnesota Magnet

Gopher tennis coach David Geatz would definitely like to see more strong Division One junior tennis players coming out of Minnesota. The new tennis complex at the university should help, but Geatz is hardly sitting back and waiting.

Using an international pipeline, fueled through word of mouth from former Gophers and from other connections, Geatz has accumulated players from such distant locations as Sweden (a constant contributor), Switzerland, India, Brazil, the Dominican Republic, Canada and Siberia, plus a wide range of locations in the United States.

Geatz expects Minnesota youth tennis to continue improving, but in the meantime, he has his Global Golden Gophers.

Number One from India

There aren't too many sophomores who already have Davis Cup competition under their belts. Harsh Mankad of Mumbai, Maharashira, India established his credentials at the University of Minnesota by being named All Big Ten Freshman of the Year and ITA Region Four Rookie of the Year in his first season. A finalist for national freshman of the year, Mankad was 31-19 in singles competition overall and 13-6 in tournament competition. Mankad paired with Jorge Duenas of the Dominican Republic for a 19- 7 doubles mark. The first freshman to play at No. 1 singles in seven years, he received the Louis Ratner Award, given to a player who has made an outstanding contribution to University of Minnesota tennis.

In the summer of 2000, Mankad went on to play for India in Davis Cup competition.*

Harsh Mankad, from Mumbai, Maharashira

Returning to the University for his sophomore year, Mankad, again No. 1 singles, was 26-12 overall and 14-7 in tournament play. He and Duenas went 10-8 in doubles.

Mankad was All Big Ten for the second straight year and was named Big Ten Sportsman of the Year, an award recognizing the highest level of sportsmanship and conduct.**

Not bad for the smallest player on the roster. Harsh Mankad is 5'8" and weighs 138 pounds.

* He also represented India in Davis Cup play in 2001.
** Mankad is the second Gopher to receive the award. Kevin Merwie won it in 1991.

Home at Last

For years, the University of Minnesota tennis program has had the use of the facilities of the Northwest Athletic Clubs. The Northwest chain has excellent accommodations, but using them required significant travel time, and court time, for good reasons, was not always available. New construction had completely wiped out the fourteen tennis courts once found on the Twin Cities campuses.

Now a new men's and women's tennis complex is being built on the Minneapolis campus, adjacent to Mariucci Arena. Containing ten indoor courts and twelve outdoor courts, the tennis program's new home will raise the level of tennis not only at the University but throughout the state.

Swimming

The Sprint and Butterfly Masters

In the early 1960s, two of the University of Minnesota's finest swimmers had overlapping careers. Steve Jackman lettered from 1961 to 1963, Wally Richardson from '63 to '65.

Jackman, from Rochester, Minnesota, the nation's best sprinter in the sixties, was All-American all three of his years. He won NCAA championships in the 100-yard freestyle in 1961 and '62 and in the 50-yard freestyle in '62 and '63. He was the Big Ten titlist in both the 50-yard and 100-yard freestyles in 1961, '62 and '63.

Richardson, from Hinsdale, Illinois, the nation's best butterfly swimmer in the sixties, was also an All-American all three of his seasons. He was the NCAA 100-yard butterfly champion in 1963 and '64 and the 200-yard butterfly winner in '64. In the Big Ten, he took the 100 crowns in 1963 and '64 and the 200 in '64.

Both Jackman and Richardson set several individual NCAA, Big Ten and Minnesota records.*

The one year their careers overlapped, 1963, they combined efforts in the four-man 400-yard relay team, helping set national records in the 400-yard medley (3:34.8) and the 400-yard freestyle medley (3:13.4).

Their careers continued to parallel after graduation. In 1986, the University of Minnesota Aquatic Hall of Fame inducted both Doctor Steven Jackman and Doctor Walter Richardson.**

* Neither swimmer was named All-Big Ten simply because such recognition was not given swimmers until 1984.
** John Bergman, from St. Paul Johnson, a Gopher All-American in 1962 and '64, also went on to become a doctor.

Dennis Dale

Dennis Dale was an outstanding swimmer for the University of Minnesota in the mid-sixtiess, earning All-American honors in the 100-meter backstroke and as the lead swimmer in the 400 medley relay.

For twelve years, Dennis coached the boys' and girls' swimming and diving teams at Burnsville, Minnesota High School, winning four state championships and earning the Coach of the Year award in each of his final four years.

Dale took over as head coach at Minnesota in 1985. The first year (5-7) was his only season with a losing record. From 1988-89 through 2000-2001, his Gopher team had an 83 percent winning average, with four Big Ten championships and eight second place finishes.

As the Gophers keep climbing nationally, with an ever-improving feeder program in the state, with the varsity program attracting more and more talented athletes nationally and internationally and with one of the world's finest facilities (the Minnesota Aquatic Center), the best is yet to come for Dennis Dale and the University of Minnesota swimming and diving program.

***Dennis Dale discusses strategy with
assistant coach Kelly Kremer***

Style Isn't Everything

When Gopher coaches watched Jay Fischer of Hutchinson, Minnesota swim, they shook their heads. He had anything but a textbook approach to the sport, and yet, "How does he manage to go so fast?"

Fischer himself had his doubts. His freshman year, he failed to make the traveling squad. Coach Dennis Dale persuaded him to keep at it for one more year. That one more year made a world of difference to Jay and to the team.

In his sophomore year, Fischer not only made the traveling squad, he was a Big Ten championship finalist. He went on to become an All-American in 1990, '91 and '92, team captain and a member of the Big Ten championship sprint relay team.

Coming Into His Own

Del Cerney of Staples, Minnesota came to the University with high expectations, both his own and his coaches'. His first two years at the U were less than impressive. Then Dennis Dale and his staff decided to treat Cerney as a team leader and to applaud his efforts in practices.

The added support worked. Del became that leader and, as a junior, won a Big Ten title in the 50-yard freestyle. In the 1992 NCAA Championships, to help the team, he gave up his best event, the 100-yard freestyle, and added the 800 freestyle relay. That's 200 yards for each relay member, but Cerney, usually a sprinter, handled it well. Cerney competed in all five relays, earned his first All-American and was a major factor in the Gophers placing sixth, their highest NCAA finish in history.

Del was an All-American three times, and was All Big Ten in 1991 and '92.

After graduating, Del Cerney, swimming for Coach Dale's Gopher Swim Club, won the 50 freestyle in the Long Course Senior Nationals, Minnesota's first win in the Nationals in over twenty years.

Recruiting Diversity

One of the keys to Dennis Dale's success is the diversity of his recruiting. His athletes come from all around the world. In the past ten years, Dale's teams have included swimmers and divers from Brazil, Malaysia, Mexico, Greece, Israel, Germany, Sweden, Norway, Canada, Finland and more, from many different states in the U. S., and, very important, the best talent from Minnesota.

Certainly the university's magnificent Aquatic Center, one of the finest facilities in the world, is a powerful attraction. Dale's winning record is another. (The number of athletes earning first team All-American honors under Dale is approaching one hundred). And when Alex Massura can come from Sao Paulo, Brazil, win All-American in four different relays as well as the 100 and 200 backstroke and twice be named Big Ten Swimmer of the Year, it does draw attention.* Other potential recruits say, "If he can do it, so can I."

As a prime example of his inspiration, Massura was Big Ten Swimmer of the Year in 1999 and 2000 but not in 2001. He continued to lead the Gophers in total points, but he no longer finished first in the backstroke every time. The reason? If he came in second or third, it was only because one or two Minnesota teammates hit the wall ahead of him.

* Massura also swam on Brazil's world record-breaking freestyle relay team.

Who Is This Kid?

When P. J. Bogart came to the University of Minnesota in 1993, he looked like he should still be in junior high school in Mesa, Arizona. Appearances can indeed be deceiving.

The diminutive Bogart was Big Ten Diver of the Year all four of his seasons, 1993, '94, '95 and '96. In his freshman year, he won the NCAA Platform Diving title. On his final dive, in an extremely tight competition, he scored 9s and 10s to come away with the crown. He now had complete national attention. It never went away. He earned All-American honors all four years and took first in the 1-meter springboard in 1995 and '96.

In the Big Ten championships, he won the title in the Platform in 1993, '94 and '95, in the 1-meter in '94, '95 and '96 and in the 3-meter in '95 and '96.

The kid from Mesa had become one of the nation's premier athletes.

After Seventy Years

In 1996, Minnesota entered the Big Ten Swimming and Diving Championships at Ann Arbor riding a string of six straight second-place finishes in the team championships. Coach Dennis Dale admitted it might be difficult to hang on to second place. Someone asked "What are our chances of winning?" Dale answered that anything was possible, but, in an aside to his staff, whispered "If we win, I'll shave my head."

The first look at the Michigan pool was disappointing. The water was a dark green color, the bottom of the pool not even visible. Several coaches from other schools complained. Dale decided not to embarrass the Michigan staff and told his Gophers to focus on the events instead.

P. J. Bogart coming off the 10-meter platform

Minnesota built a good lead the first day, but the morning paper the next day quoted a swimmer from favored Michigan as saying, "Minnesota has done that before, but from here on, it's going to be all Michigan."

From there on, it was all Minnesota. The Gophers expanded their lead on day two and stretched it even more the final day. The University of Minnesota had won its first Big Ten Swimming and Diving championship in seventy years. (The only other wins had been in 1923 and 1926.)

In the post-tournament celebration, Dennis got the usual coach's toss into the pool, but he didn't have to shave his head. His staff, grudgingly, kept his whispered aside a secret.

A Huge Splash

On February 20, 2001, I attended a media conference at which Dennis Dale discussed his team's chances later that week in the Big Ten Swimming and Diving Championships, to be held at the University's Aquatic Center. In 1996, Dale had not expected to win, but the Gophers sprang a major upset. In 1998, taking the title was somewhat less of a surprise. This time, Dale was optimistic but cautioned, "We may be behind after Thursday's first round, but if it's no more than 60 points, we should be all right."

60 points behind? After day one, Minnesota led second-place Penn State by 71 points!

After day two, Penn State and Michigan, tied for second, were 171 points back. In two days, Minnesota already had virtually clinched the crown.

The Gophers did not let up. They finished 248 points ahead of second-place Michigan. Their 797 points became the highest total in twenty-seven years.

Minnesota swimmers shattered conference and school records left and right, with twelve Gophers named to the All Big Ten Team. Dan Croaston swept the Big Ten diving awards and was named Big Ten Diver of the Year. His coach, KZ Li, was named Big Ten Diving Coach of the Year. To complete the sweep, Dennis Dale was named Big Ten Coach of the Year.

The sign and the joy say it all

Gymnastics

Thirty Years and More

When Fred Roethlisberger took over as head coach for Minnesota men's gymnastics in 1972, the Gophers had finished better than fourth in the Big Ten only once in seventeen years (a second-place finish in 1960). Roethlisberger made an immediate impact. The U of M was third in the conference in 1972, '73 and '74. In 1975, it moved up a notch to second.

Then came a remarkable stretch. In 1976, Minnesota won its first Big Ten title since 1949. First place suddenly became a habit. From '76 through 1980, the Gophers topped the conference five years in a row. Fred's teams took first again in 1982, '84, '90, '91, '92 and '95. In a span of twenty years, Roethlisberger's squads had won the Big Ten crown eleven times, with five second-place finishes.

Fred has coached twenty-one All-Americans, has been named Big Ten Coach of the Year four times, United States Gymnastics Federation Coach of the Year four times and Midwest Region Coach of the Year five times.

2002 marks the one-hundredth anniversary of University of Minnesota gymnastics, and Fred Roethlisberger feels it may mark another upward swing in his teams' fortunes.

May the Best Man Win

Jay Lowinske came to Gopher gymnastics from New Ulm, Minnesota. Tim LaFleur checked in from Milwaukee, Wisconsin. They began and maintained a "Minnesota versus Wisconsin" rivalry. The rivalry led to a permanent friendship.

LaFleur got the honors, but Lowinske contributed significantly to Fred Roethlisberger's first three Big Ten championships (1976-1978). In addition, the two gymnasts, in their rivalry, pushed each other to higher standards.

Tim and Jay were the best men at each other's weddings. A double victory.

The Halftime Show

I first saw Marie and John Roethlisberger in action in 1972. They performed with their father, Fred, at the halftime of a Gopher basketball game. I had trouble concentrating on my halftime statistics because I was fascinated by the strength and coordination of these two little kids. Marie was seven years old. Lying on her back, this little girl supported her father (his hands on her knees) while he did a shoulder stand on her arms. The performance ended with John (four years younger than Marie) joining his sister and father in a three-person forward roll (A holds B's ankles, B holds C's ankles, C holds A's ankles, and they roll and roll and roll).

It was an indication of what was to come. Marie and John went on to become world class gymnasts.*

* Marie is now a doctor in Madison, Wisconsin.

The Nissen Award

The most prestigious individual award in collegiate gymnastics is the Nissen Award. Named after George Nissen, a three-time NCAA champion at the University of Iowa, it is given each year to the most outstanding senior gymnast in the United States.

Two U of M gymnasts have received the Nissen Award. The first was Tim LaFleur in 1978. The Milwaukee gymnast had five Big Ten titles with the Gophers: the 1977 horizontal bar, the 1977 still rings, and, in 1976, '77 and '78, the conference all-around. He was also a member of the 1978 and '79 United States teams in the World Championships.

Tim's older brother, Jeff LaFleur, also starred for the Gophers, winning the Big Ten parallel bars in 1976.

The other Nissen Award winner was John Roethlisberger in 1993. John, a three-time Olympian, won the NCAA parallel bars title in 1991, the pommel horse in 1993 and the NCAA all-around championships three straight years, 1991, '92 and '93.*

John Roethlisberger

In the Big Ten, John won four straight all-arounds, two parallel bar titles, and championships in the horizontal bar, pommel horse and vault. With the U. S. National team, Roethlisberger was a four-time all-around king.

Tim LaFleur and John Roethlisberger—two very worthy recipients of the Nissen Award.

* The only other NCAA all-around champion from Minnesota was Newt Loken, winning in 1942. Loken also placed first in the NCAA horizontal bars in 1941.

The First 21st Century All-American

As a freshman, Clay Strother took part in all gymnastic events, advancing to the NCAA championship round in the pommel horse. As a sophomore, his marks improved dramatically. Then in the final dual meet of the season, against Nebraska, Strother sprained an ankle, a bad sprain. That day, he was only able to compete in two events. Two weeks later, in the Big Ten tournament, the injury limited his participation to just four events, and these, for Strother, were subpar performances.

However, the ankle improved, and Clay Strother's determination never wavered. He qualified for the NCAA Championships. He finished fifth in the all-around (the top six earn All-American status), and the next night, he won first place in the floor exercise and the pommel horse. Less than a month after his injury, Clay Strother had become a three-time All-American and in 2001, the only gymnast with two event firsts.

The young man from Jasper, Texas, has listed "coming to the University of Minnesota" as his biggest sports thrill. Minnesota gymnastics is thrilled to have him here.

Clay Strother

Fred's "Most Satisfying" List

Fred Roethlisberger's first thirty years have included many satisfactions. Among them:

His first Big Ten title in 1976.

Having Tim LaFleur and John Roethlisberger win the Nissen Award and make the United State National Teams.

His most inspirational team members—son John and Dan Zimpfer. Zimpfer, who won the Big Ten floor exercise in 1990, was not as gifted an athlete as John, but both had a mental strength that has meant a great deal to their coach.*

Having seven of his athletes win the Big Ten Conference Medal of Honor for excellence both as a student and as an athlete (Jeff and Tim LaFleur, Brian Meeker, Joey Ray, Collen Godkin, John Roethlisberger and Brian Yee).

The way Gopher athletes from elsewhere in the nation stay on in the Twin Cities area after graduation.

Fred Roethlisberger is still aiming for an NCAA team championship, the one title that has eluded him. That would make his "Most Satisfying" list complete.

* Dan Zimpfer died in a mountain-climbing accident in Colorado in the late 1990s.

Fred Roethlisberger supporting son John

Track and Field
and
Cross Country

Magic with the Discus

Fortune Gordien was Minnesota's King of the Discus in the 1940s. In 1943, Gordien won both the Big Ten Discus and Shot Put titles. Returning after World War II, he repeated as discus champion in 1947 and '48 and earned All-American status by finishing first in the NCAA discus competition in 1946, '47 and '48. Gordien went on to compete in three Olympics, capturing two discus medals, the bronze in 1948 and the silver in 1956.

Gordien's father was the famous magician The Great Gordon, and on a lesser scale, his son followed in his footsteps. Fortune Gordien appeared in some Hollywood cowboy movies. I saw one of them. It included a minor role which must have been created for Fortune. He played a cowboy who specialized in card tricks. No discus throwing, though.

Coach Roy Griak, then a student member of the track team, recalls a Gopher trip to Lincoln, Nebraska, for a meet with the Cornhuskers. Fortune Gordien talked a Nebraska fan into giving him a half dollar, warning him that if the fan couldn't figure out how Gordien made the coin disappear, the fifty cents would not be returned. Disappear it did, and, as far as Roy knows, the Nebraskan is still fifty cents poorer.

A National Title with Two Unexpected Contributions

In 1948 at Minnesota's Memorial Stadium, Jim Kelly's team gave Minnesota its only NCAA track and field championship with two of its point-getters competing in their event for the first time. Lloyd LaMois was the big hero with a first place finish in the Hop, Step and Jump (soon to be renamed the Triple Jump). He had never before competed in the event in competition.

An even more unlikely point-getter was football and wrestling star Leo Nomellini. Coach Kelly located Nomellini at his fraternity house and persuaded Leo the Lion to give it his best in the Hammer Throw. Leo's throw was good for eighth place, which earned him one point. Minnesota won the national title-by one point.*

* The 1948 NCAA track and field championships marked my first play-by-play broadcasts. KUOM carried my periodic reports from Memorial Stadium. Some of them were long enough that I could describe a complete event. I had no idea that I would ever broadcast play-by-play again.

Photo Finish

In 1968, at Memorial Stadium, Roy Griak's track and field squad won the Big Ten title. Michigan was the big favorite, but Minnesota kept it close.

Day one of the two-day event had been warm and sunny. Day two was cold and rainy. The championship was decided in the 200-meter relay. Official Ted Hass told coach Griak he felt Gopher Rich Simonsen had hit the tape first, and Hass had a keen eye. (Griak says Hass could watch eight runners in a tight finish and immediately, and correctly, list the order of finish.)

Hass proved to be right, but the final tournament results were withheld until the 16-millimeter film of the race could be developed.

On day three, it was announced that Minnesota had won the 4 x 200 (in a school record time of 1:24.5) and, by one point, the Gophers were the Big Ten champions.

The Nation's Largest Cross-Country Invitational

Roy Griak served as head coach for Minnesota's cross-country and track and field team from 1963 to 1995. His thirty-three seasons included two Big Ten cross-country titles (1964 and 1969) and a 1968 conference track and field crown. In 1993, he was

Roy Griak, left, confers with Phil Lundin

named to the Drake Relays Coaches Hall of Fame. In December of 2001, he was inducted into the U.S. Track Coaches Hall of Fame. When Griak stepped down as head coach in 1996, the Minnesota Cross-Country Invitational was renamed the Griak Invitational. In typical Griak fashion, he made the September event the largest of its kind in the nation. It brings in about one hundred men's and one hundred women's college and high school teams.

Roy Griak, as administrative assistant for the cross-country and track and field departments, continues to be a vital force in the sports he loves so well.

Twig's Most Prominent Native Son

Garry Bjorklund comes from the tiny northern Minnesota community of Twig (located a few miles north of Duluth). His achievements in track and field and cross-country would fill a Twig billboard to overflowing.

In track, Garry Bjorklund set Big Ten indoor records in the 3,000-meter and the two-mile in 1970 and, in 1972, in the 5,000-meter and three-mile.

He posted conference outdoor track marks in 1971 in the mile, three-mile and six-mile.

Bjorklund captured the NCAA six-mile title in 1971.

In cross-country, Bjorklund finished first in the Big Ten in 1969, '70 and '71. He won the conference five-mile crown in 1969 and '70 and the six-mile in '71.

Garry Bjorklund holds fourteen different University of Minnesota records.

Steve Plasencia's Gopher career was just beginning when Bjorklund's U of M career was coming to an end. For a brief time, they were roommates, and Steve feels that was an inspiring jumpstart to his own achievements.

Garry Bjorklund, long distance champion

Going Cross-Country? Double Your Miles

Steve Plasencia has had six successful seasons as the Gopher cross-country coach. In just his second season, he led the Gophers to their first NCAA appearance in sixteen years. They keep coming back.

There are several reasons for their success. Plasencia's credentials as a runner are top-flight. He was a three-time cross-country All American and two-time track All American from 1976 to 1978. And he's still running. In 1998, he broke his own American Masters half-marathon record and the Masters 10,000 meter mark.*

As a coach, he has his twenty or so cross-country runners practice and compete with the track team, starting in January and continuing for six months. When the cross-country events begin in September, they are very ready. (It helps that Plasencia is Phil Lundin's assistant in track and field.)

* Steve Placensia's biggest thrill in three decades of running: representing the United States in the 10,000 meters in the 1988 Olympics in Seoul, South Korea.

1998 — Inside-Outside

In Phil Lundin's first six years as Minnesota's track and field coach, the Gophers have never finished lower than third place in the Big Ten indoor championships and never below second in the conference outdoor championships. Coming into Lundin's first season, 1996, Minnesota, in a near-century of Big Ten competition, had only two outdoor titles (1948 and 1968) and no indoor crowns.

In 1997, Minnesota had three individual titles in the indoor championships but finished third in the team standings. 1998

*All-American runner Andrew McKessock (left) with
cross-country coach Steve Plasencia*

brought only two individual crowns (Staffan Strand in the high jump and Benjamin Jensen with a Big Ten and school record in the heptathlon), but with fourteen Gophers finishing in the top five overall, Minnesota's depth gave the team its first Big Ten title ever.

The outdoor conference championships were held almost three months later. As with the indoor title, Minnesota ended Wisconsin's three-year reign as champion and again won the crown with great depth (twelve finishers in the top five) and just two individual winners. Football cornerback Fred Rodgers took the 100-meter dash with a career-best time of 10.44. Staffan Strand won the high jump, repeating his triumph at the indoor championships.

Minnesota also won the Big Ten outdoor championship in 1999, and Phil Lundin earned back-to-back Conference Coach of the Year honors in '98 and '99.

Phil Lundin celebrates with the 1998 Big Ten champions

A Home-Grown Four by Four

Phil Lundin is proud that so many of his track and field athletes are from Minnesota, and he cites the 2001 4x4 1600 meter relay team as a prime example. The four, plus one alternate, won the Big Ten title with a school record time of 3:04.12. The members include Mitch Potter of Isanti, Minnesota; Tom Gerding of Waconia, MN; Andy Wohlin of Saint Paul, MN and Mikael Jakobsson of Orebro, Sweden; plus alternate Adam Steele of Eden Prairie, MN.

The unit finished fifth in the NCAA, earning All-American honors.

Memorial Stadium — the Track, the Field, the Man

From the Bernie Bierman era through the 1960s, Virg Dwinell was the Memorial Stadium Groundskeeper. He kept the football field in as nearly perfect a condition as anyone could imagine.

The track, which encircled the football field, was not the usual cinder track of those days, but rather was made of crushed brick. Roy Griak recalls getting to his office at 6:30 a.m. most days. By then, Virg would already have the track dragged, rolled (with a mammoth roller) and lined. His work ethic was without parallel.

How about singing the Rouser for unsung hero Virg Dwinell?

Traditions

"Pinky"

In the 1940s, Richard McNamara was one of five boys brought up by their mother in Hastings, Minnesota. Times were tough. Clothes had to last. Dick's red corduroy pants lasted very well, but they faded, and that's where the nickname "Pinky" began and stuck. Even today, I call him Dick most of the time, but occasionally a "Pinky" slips in.

Two Hastings High School grads-
Dick "Pinky" McNamara and Ben Utecht

"Pinky" and older brother Bob started in the same Gopher backfield in 1954 (see "The 1 and 2 Return"). Dick had an inter-departmental major he put together himself. It needed the help of an outstanding adviser. He had two of the best-first Vivian Hewer, then Mabel Powers. He never forgot them. In 1992, McNamara, now the very successful chairman of the Activar Corporation, made a sizeable donation to the advising program of the College of Liberal Arts.

In 1998, he gave ten million dollars to the University, with the money designated for the liberal arts program, for intercolle-

The Memorial Stadium Main Arch,
now at home in the McNamara Center

giate athletics and to help complete an alumni and visitor's center. That center has been named the McNamara Alumni Center. Among its occupants is the University of Minnesota Board of Regents. Richard "Pinky" McNamara is a member of that board.

The exterior of the alumni center's geode construction is covered with 40,000 square feet of rose-colored granite blocks. In just the right light, they look pink.

Spirit!

Cheerleaders and dance-line performers at Gopher athletic events have become such an integral part of the event that we tend to overlook the fact that these are athletes in their own right. Because they don't fall under NCAA rules, they practice more hours than football, basketball and other players. With special appearances, practice hours can average 700 a year.* At Minnesota, there are no spirit squad scholarships, but squad participants must maintain qualifying grade averages, similar to those of other athletes.

The Gopher cheerleaders at Williams Arena

Beth Frees, in charge of spirit squad events, has been a cheerleader, then a director of cheerleaders, then a dance line director. She says that typically, each April, fifty applicants vie for the sixteen dance line positions. Almost all will have had several years of dance studio training.

Sam Owens, the head cheer coach, also expects about fifty women to audition for the ten cheerleader positions. Usually, only about twenty men try out for the ten male spots.

In addition to high school cheerleading, the women often have gymnastics backgrounds. They average 5'1", 105 pounds, because, according to Beth, "they get thrown around a lot."

As high school cheer teams are usually all-female, men are harder to find. Their size varies, but Owens says the wrestler physique is ideal, with gymnastics a close second. (Sam has started an all-girls squad, giving more women an opportunity to participate. It appears at football and basketball games.)

Hockey cheerleaders are chosen separately. Here the women don't get tossed around, but obviously, skating ability is paramount.

All spirit squad members have a required strength and conditioning program, which reduces injuries considerably. All must have positive, friendly personalities.

The annual national competition is held in Orlando, Florida. The dance line and cheerleading squad each send in a video tape. The ranking each tape receives determines whether that squad is invited to the nationals. Since 1993, the University of Minnesota dance lines and cheerleaders have received invitations each year. During those years, the dance line has averaged a top ten finish, the cheerleaders a top sixteen, both very high ratings.

In recent years, the total membership of the several squads has grown from thirty-five to seventy-five, the coaches from one to eight. The coaches are members of the AACCA, the American Association of Cheering Coaches and Advisors. The Big Ten sets the performance standards for eleven schools. At the university, a spirit squad booster club has begun, and it's growing. Seventy-five alumni participated in the 2001 Homecoming festivities.

The most recognizable member of the spirit team is Goldy Gopher. There used to be just one Goldy, but the demand for the

JACQUELINE SINCLAIRE is a Toronto-based writer by profession but erotic by nature. Her work has appeared in *Lips Like Sugar*; *Naughty Stories from A to Z*, volume 4; and *Velvet Heat*. A firm believer that sex and masturbation are both healthy and necessary, she considers it her civic duty to write smut. The rest is up to you.

SAGE VIVANT operates Custom Erotica Source, where she writes tailor-made erotic fiction for individual clients. She is the author of *Your Erotic Personality* and the novel *Giving the Bride Away*. With coeditor M. Christian, she has edited *Confessions*; *The Best of Both Worlds*; *Amazons*; *Garden of the Perverse*; and *Leather, Lace and Lust*. Her stories have appeared in numerous anthologies.

SASKIA WALKER (www.saskiawalker.co.uk) is a British author who has had erotic fiction published on both sides of the pond. You can find her work in many anthologies, including most recently *Best Women's Erotica 2006*; *Red Hot Erotica*;*Slave to Love*; *Secrets*, volume 15; *The Mammoth Book of Best New Erotica*, volume 5; and *Stirring Up a Storm*. Her longer work includes the novels *Along for the Ride* and *Double Dare*.

MARK WILLIAMS is a fortysomething married Chicagoan who is versatile, if nothing else. He has written everything from promotional material for Trump Plaza in Atlantic City to sketches for the WGN-TV children's program *The Bozo Show*. He's been a correspondent/researcher for *Playboy* magazine for many years, and he is a polished professional stand-up comedian as well. His short stories have appeared in *Best Bondage Erotica*, *Down & Dirty*, and *Naughty Stories from A to Z*, volume 2.

"Goldy"

mascot has become so large that there are now five. Many schools have mascots with fierce, haughty expressions. Goldy is active but with a very friendly face and demeanor. Kids love Goldy. What more can you ask?

Let's hear it for Goldy! And let's have the cheer led by the only athletic group at the university in which men and women work together to achieve a victory in their event.

* The practice and performance schedule of the University Marching Band is also a demanding one, similar to that of the spirit squads (see "Dr. Ben" and "The Band").

Freeze the Action

Wendell Vandersluis and Jerry Lee are the photographers for a majority of the pictures in this book. Wendell wielded his cameras with skill for just over thirty years for Gopher Men's Athletics. When Wendell retired, Jerry, already in place as a U of M sports photographer, took over the top spot, with Michelle King as his assistant.

Asked for their most memorable images, Vandersluis and Lee both chose a crowd setting. Wendell looks back to the 1977 shutout of Michigan, 16-0, at Memorial Stadium. The Gopher crowd did not want to leave the stadium, unwilling to break the spell of a major upset. As Wendell thinks back, "They just stood around."

Jerry remembers the jam-packed crowd at Williams Arena in 1997, waiting to welcome the basketball Gophers on their return home from San Antonio, where victories over Clemson and UCLA had put them into the Final Four. When the team finally arrived at midnight, the crowd erupted, and the eruptions kept repeating for many minutes (see "Midnight Madness").

The toughest sport to cover? Wendell goes back to the days when cameras required the photographer to constantly change focus, and that made football, with its many players and sudden shifting field position, the most difficult. Available photographers were assigned areas and tasks best suited to their aptitudes, but there were always unexpected surprises.

For Jerry, even with today's advanced equipment, nailing a goal being scored in hockey or a punt being blocked in football are the biggest challenges.

Both photographers have been knocked down at the sideline or baseline in football or basketball. Jerry recalls running back Chris Darkins catapulting out of bounds but having the presence of mind to scoop up Lee and shield him from injury when they hit the turf.

Vandersluis was actually knocked unconscious while covering a spring football scrimmage. Wendell didn't see an official running full speed. The official didn't see Wendell. Moments later, trainer Doug Locy swam into Wendell's blurred vision, asking questions. "I was still a little groggy that night," says Wendell.

Of all the athletes Wendell snapped in his three decades, basketball star Willie Burton heads the "most fun" list. After a victory, Burton had a boyish joy that went far beyond just being photogenic.

Away from sports, photography is also a hobby for both Jerry Lee and Wendell Vandersluis. Jerry enjoys photographing soaring red-tailed hawks and is considering eagles. Wendell and his wife Cindy like to travel, and he does take along a camera or two.

Longtime Coaches

In an era when coaches are so often hired only to be fired, it's refreshing to note a few who not only survived but achieved memorable results. These are in no particular order, but all coached for thirty or more years at the University of Minnesota.

Wally Johnson, the wrestling coach for thirty-four years, from 1952-53 to 1985-86, had a Gopher career mark of 390-207-11. A member of the National Wrestling Hall of Fame, Wally also served as an assistant Gopher football coach from 1956 to 1963.

Niels Thorpe was the swimming coach for thirty-seven years, from 1920-21 to 1956-57. He led the Gophers to two Big Ten titles and eight second place finishes.

Les Bolstad was the golf coach for thirty years, from 1947 to 1976. In 1983, the University of Minnesota Golf Course was renamed the Les Bolstad Golf Course. (See "Yes Sir, Mr. Bolstad.")

Roy Griak was the track and field and cross-country coach for thirty-three years, from 1963 to 1995. (See "The Nation's Largest Cross-Country Invitational.")

Dr. Ralph Piper was the gymnastics coach for thirty-seven years (all but five years during the period 1930-1971). He coached his teams to six Big Ten championships, two second-place finishes in the NCAA and was National Coach of the Year in 1962.

Fred Roethlisberger has been the men's gymnastics coach since 1972 and is still going strong. (See "Fred's Most Satisfying List")

Dick Siebert was the baseball coach for thirty-one years, from 1948 to 1978. (See "How to Follow a Tough Act to Follow")

A special nod to George "Butch" Nash who was an assistant football coach for thirty-four years, from 1947 to 1980 then a volunteer assistant for eight years, from 1984 to 1991.

Another nod to Lloyd "Snapper" Stein, a trainer for thirty-seven years, from 1935 to 1975, with four years away in the navy during World War II. "Snapper" is a member of the Helm Hall of Fame, recognizing outstanding achievement as a trainer.

And finally, here's to Jim Marshall, approaching forty years as a trainer and training facilities administrator.

Fog

In my final three years of football play-by-play, I partnered with Darrell Thompson and Dave Mona. Now they have joined Dave Lee in an excellent broadcast team.

I sat at home, listening to their description of the Minnesota-Northwestern game at Evanston, October 13, 2001. A heavy fog at Ryan Field made any description difficult.

A kickoff appeared to go into the end zone.

Dave Mona's analysis:

"It sounded long."

The Pancake Prediction

On October 20, 2001, the first season of my retirement, Bobby Bell and I were the grand marshals for the homecoming parade preceding the Minnesota-Michigan State game. Immediately after the parade, I interviewed Bobby as part of a pregame pancake breakfast (the game had an 11:10 a.m. kickoff time). Following that, I guided eight young "play-by-play" aspirants through a scripted "Gopher touchdown" against Michigan State.

In the script, with "two minutes left," Ron Johnson caught a touchdown pass and "Minnesota widens its lead to 27 to 19."

Now, let's assume, in this scripted fantasy, that Minnesota made the extra point. That would make the score 28-19.

A little more than an hour later, Minnesota and Michigan State met at the Metrodome. I watched the Gophers win the game.

Ron Johnson caught a touchdown pass.

The final score was Minnesota 28 - Michigan State 19.

2000-2001 — Lasting Memories

When I look back at my final football and basketball seasons, I realize that my most vivid memories are not only of the games, but equally of the warm friendships made through those games:

Gopher tackle Adam Haayer and his pride in having me meet his family.

Gopher guard Derek Burns. He never failed to say "Hi" or to nod and smile.

Gopher assistant football coach Vic Adamle. He always went out of his way to shake hands and chat.

Gopher basketball player Trevor Winter. I did the readings when he and Heidi married, a very emotional experience for me.

Gopher basketball players Terrance Simmons and Randy Chall, both with firm handshakes before and after each game, win or lose. Simmons had the most playing minutes on the squad, Chall possibly the fewest. The handshakes were equally important.

Gopher basketball player John-Blair Bickerstaff. J-B was always already at Williams Arena, shooting baskets and free throws, when I arrived two hours before tipoff. As I made my way to my broadcast location in the upper deck, Bickerstaff would always turn, look up and wave. I would always wave back.

When J-B's Gopher career ended with a broken leg, he went to Denver for surgery, but he left word with one of the student managers to seek me out before the next home game. The manager did, and gave me a wave, saying, "This is from J-B."

I waved back.

Signoff

It seems appropriate to conclude this book with the closing words following my final play-by-play March 19, 2001. The last five words are the out-cue for the closing commercial billboard, but they too seem fitting.

"So, we come to the end of my principal profession for half a century, broadcasting what goes on in a sports event. Fifty years and 510 games of University of Minnesota football, 45 years and 1,309 games of Gopher basketball. A lot of other games—high school, college, professional.

"This has been a wonderful and rewarding part of my life, but it's never the only part. I'm ready to move on.

"One thing more—broadcasting is, or at least should be, one person trying to communicate something to one other person, not a specific person. I hope I have reached you.

"And, as always, I thank you for listening.

"This is Golden Gopher Sports."

Epilogue

Save Gopher Sports

Just about the same time the first edition of this book was rolling off the presses, dark financial clouds were forming over the Gopher sports program.

The scandal surrounding the basketball program's NCAA violations still dominated the news coverage in 2000. In the final month of 1999 President Mark Yudof appointed his trusted aide Tonya Moten Brown to oversee the athletic department, which had most recently reported to former Athletics Director McKinley Boston. One of Yudof's first promises to the Board of Regents was that Moten Brown would do a thorough review of the financial outlook for the Men's and Women's separate athletics departments.

Everyone feared the report would be negative, but no one anticipated the size of the projected shortfall.

Moten Brown told Regents that the departments, soon to be merged under incoming Athletics Director Joel Maturi, would face a shortfall of some $31 million over the next few years. The Regents asked for a plan and Yudof and Moten Brown proposed a plan to eliminate three teams, men's gymnastics and women's and men's golf.

About the same time, the State of Minnesota received a forecast of a $4.56 billion deficit over the next biennium. Everyone, including the University, would have to share the pain.

But not so fast. A group of influential alumni, many of them former athletes, asked President Yudof for a specific amount of money that would be needed to save the three threatened sports. Bob McNamara and Harvey Mackay learned the magic number was $2.7 million, and it had to be in the bank by Jan. 31, 2003.

"Save Gopher Sports" was begun, and the mood began to change almost immediately. Former athletes stepped forward to endow scholarships, to provide not only a temporary but also a long-term solution.

Tom Lehman, the most famous Minnesota Gopher golfer in history, came home to host a golf event. With a few personal calls from the 1996 British Open champion, every slot quickly sold out. KARE 11 TV and WCCO combined efforts on a radio/telethon that raised an astounding $654,244 in one afternoon and evening.

The entire $2.7 million was in hand the last week of January and President Yudof congratulated Gopher fans for stepping up. The program to drop the three sports was scrapped and the department learned several important lessons that would be put to use again later in the decade.

Par for the Course

The annals of college golf in the United States have long been dominated by the warm-weather states, whose golfers play the game in their own backyards some 365 days a year. Since 1956, Houston has won 16 NCAA team championships. Since 1963, Oklahoma State has won 10 times.

Over the past 51 years, the list of Big Ten winners is short. Purdue, hosting the event in 1961, scored a surprise victory, while medalist honors went to Ohio States' young Jack Nicklaus. The Buckeyes won the team championship in 1979. Minnesota had been pretty much a non-factor at the team championships, although James McLean took individual honors in 1998.

    In the summer of 2002 the Gopher men's and women's
golf teams were playing under the shadow of elimination...not
from an event, but from existence. Their teams were two of the
three targeted for elimination. Players were told there would be
no penalties or loss of eligibility if they were to transfer at the end
of the season. Most of them realized this would most likely be the
final season of intercollegiate golf at Minnesota.

    Might as well make the best of it.

    Their head coach, Brad James, carried the actual title of
Interim Head Coach. No hurry to name a head coach when the
program is going away.

    The teams, with no big names such as McLean, played
well throughout the season. Still, it was a surprise to many when
they qualified for the NCAA Championship at Ohio State.

    Coach James recalled the circumstances. "We were not
expected to win. Everyone thinks we can't play because we're a
Big Ten school and we play in the North. Nothing is ever written about us having a chance to win. We expect to win. We know
we can do it. Everyone's expectations of schools up North is that
Northern teams can't play. We had no pressure and we had nothing to lose."

    The media coverage leading up to the event made no
mention of the Gophers, except for a small note that the team had
been targeted for elimination.

    The Gophers played reasonably well the first two days,
but outplayed every other team in the field on Friday, moving into
fourth place in the process.

    All of the sudden the media noticed. This was David vs.
Goliath.

    With all eyes on them Saturday, the team didn't disap-
point. Coach James had golfers at various points around the
course. The leader board was slow to keep up. A par here. A birdie
there. All over the course he was starting to receive congratulations
as the Gophers surged into the lead.

    Junior Matt Anderson led Minnesota with a final round
of 66. With all the pressure on him and the team, Anderson shot

the best round of any Gopher in any event in the last two years. His teammate, sophomore Justin Smith, shot 69 on the final day and finished tied for fourth place at 5-under 279. Anderson finished in a tie for eighth at 281.

Junior Wilhelm Schauman shot 71 in the final round, and sophomore David Morgan was just one shot back at 72.

The underdog Gophers, huge fan favorites in the final round, fired a team score of 6-under 278 on the final round to defeat second-place Georgia Tech by five shots. The Gophers were the only team to finish the championship below par.

Back in the Twin Cities the made-for-Hollywood story did not go unnoticed. It was the featured story in both the Minneapolis and St. Paul sports sections, and the fledgling "Save Gopher Sports" effort got off to a great start.

Lindsay Whalen, Game Changer

Record books may indicate the birth of the women's athletics program at the University of Minnesota as July 1975, but the program first drew the attention of a major audience some 15 years later with the arrival of a point guard from Hutchinson, Minnesota, named Lindsay Whalen.

Despite the fact that Whalen led her high school team to three consecutive conference championships and was a fourtime All State Honorable Mention selection, her decision to attend Minnesota went essentially unnoticed. Such was the state of the women's basketball team at the time.

Cheryl Littlejohn was Whalen's coach in the 2000-01 campaign. The team played in the Pavilion end of Williams Arena to crowds as small as 400 fans, mostly friends and family. While Whalen's play was spectacular, the team languished, finishing just 8-20 and winning only one of 16 Big Ten games. Littlejohn's record at the time was 29-81 and 7-57 in conference games.

Gopher women's basketball dipped to an all-time low

when Littlejohn was dismissed after an NCAA investigation alleged that she had paid a needy player $200 to $300 and had run practices outside of NCAA approved times.

Enter Brenda Oldfield, a young, but promising coach who inherited Whalen and a freshman center from Wisconsin, whose real name was Janel McCarville and who, knowingly overweight, gladly responded to the nickname of Shaq.

One of Oldfield's first jobs was to evaluate her returning talent. In Whalen, she found a player who scored 15 points and a team-leading seven rebounds in her first game as a freshman. The next day she scored 27 and was named the MVP of the Sheraton Four Points Classic. A month later, she scored 31 against Northwestern.

In Whalen, Oldfield had a point guard. What remained was to establish a mission, confidence, and an inside game.

Whalen found a strange mix of freedom and discipline under Coach Oldfield. The few fans there for pre-season games saw a poised leader dribbling slowly at the top of the key with her right hand as she used her left to guide her teammates into proper positions away from the basket. Whalen had just what she needed... a path to the basket blocked only by a single defender who seemed helpless to stop what was coming.

Whalen would drive the right side, initiate contact, and use a reverse spin to gain leverage on the defender. From that point she would either bank in a shot or make a perfect pass to the driving McCarville. Either option proved to be nearly unstoppable.

That move was one of two that would resonate with fans even a decade later. The other came when teams were foolish enough to challenge Whalen on a man-to-man press.

Whalen would toy with the defender, leading her ever closer to a planted McCarville. At just the right time Whalen would execute a quick pivot and streak past her teammate. Time and again the defender would realize too late that she was on a collision course for McCarville. As the hapless defender wobbled to the floor, McCarville would jog down court to take place in a lethal game of five on four before the officials could stop play to attend to the senseless defender.

On a January trip to Wisconsin, the basketball world began to notice this team. Wisconsin was ranked #5 in the nation and had sold a remarkable 17,600 tickets to welcome the usually docile Gophers.

Not this time.

Led by Whalen and McCarville, a Wisconsin high school legend, the Gophers pulled the game out in the last minute.

While that was happening in Madison, a pipe broke inside the Pavilion end of Williams Arena, making the women's court unplayable. The way to continue the home season was to join the men in the larger arena. For many years Gopher Women's Athletic Director Chris Voelz denied playing a role in the pipe breaking.

Nevertheless, the women were on page one in both local newspapers as they returned home, ranked in the NCAA Top 25 for the first time in history. Their first game in Williams Arena drew a record 11,389 fans.

With Oldfield as coach, the team improved from 8-20 to 22-8. Oldfield was named Associated Press' Coach of the Year and promptly announced she was leaving Minnesota for Maryland.

Under Whalen's charismatic leadership, attendance at Gopher women's basketball rose from an average of 1,087 her freshman year to 9,866 her senior year.

She led her team to its only Final Four appearance in 2004. By the time she graduated she held the team record in points, scoring average, games in double figures, free throws made, and free throw percentage. She became the only four-time team MVP in school history and was a three-time All-American.

She was a first-round WNBA draft choice of the Connecticut Sun and was traded to the Minnesota Lynx in 2010 and led her team to the WNBA title a year later. In 2012 she won a gold medal as a member of the U.S. Olympic team in London. At the beginning of the 2013 season the Lynx acquired Janel McCarville in a trade, once again linking the two top performers in Gopher women's basketball history.

Perfection

It just doesn't happen that often... and when it does, it's something to note and long remember.

Ask more fans what they think of when it comes to a perfect season, and they'll most likely respond with the Miami Dolphins, 17-0 in 1972. If they are college basketball fans they may recall the run of UCLA teams in the 1960s and Indiana in 1976. College football plays too few games to count and professional baseball, basketball, and hockey play too many. Even the 1927 New York Yankees, perhaps the best baseball team ever, finished the season with a 110-44 record.

They may have had Babe Ruth, Lou Gehrig, and Tony Lazzeri, but they didn't have Amanda Kessel, Noora Raty, and Hannah Brandt.

The 2012-13 Gopher Women's Hockey team was special from the start. Not only were they the defending national champions, but they had almost a perfect blend of veterans and rookies.

How good was this team that finished a remarkable 41-0 en route to the NCAA title? They not only were perfect, but they rolled up some stats that may never again be approached.

For instance, they trailed for a total of only 50 minutes and 42 seconds in the entire year. That's more than nine minutes less than *60 Minutes*. By Gopher standards we would never have gotten to know Andy Rooney.

Amanda Kessel scored 46 goals over the 41-game season. All opponents combined scored 36. Brandt, a freshman, had 33.

Kessel won every award in women's hockey except best goaltender, and Raty won that one.

Kessel, who followed her brother, Phil, to Minnesota, received the Patty Kazmaier Award (women's version of the Hobey Baker), USA Player of the Year, and Big Ten Female Athlete of the Year. Brandt, the freshman from Hill Murray, was an obvious choice for WCHA Rookie of the Year.

The Gophers, led by coach Brad Frost (Frosty to his players), beat Boston University 6-3 in the championship game before a standing-room-only crowd on home ice at Ridder Arena.

Back to Campus

Glen Mason loved to tell the story.

A top prospect was coming to town and he was eager to show the young man where he would be playing football for the next four years.

So he called the Metrodome and they said, "Feel free to bring him over. We've got a great Tractor Pull tonight."

"I didn't want to show him a Tractor Pull. I wanted to show him a football field. Our football field. But it really wasn't our football field."

While Mason, Men's Athletics Director Tom Moe, and a few others talked openly about bringing Gopher football back to campus (it had fled to the Metrodome in 1982), the public debate began in 2000 as an economic review of the finances of the athletic department cited the Metrodome as a major impediment to maximizing football revenues.

A plan for a joint on-campus facility for both the Gophers and Vikings was proposed in 2002, but the sides could not agree on a plan and the idea was abandoned the next year.

In September 2003 businessman T. Denny Sanford burst on the scene with a promise to personally fund an on-campus stadium. While that plan never came to fruition, the University, under President Bob Bruininks, emerged from discussions totally dedicated to getting the job done.

In March 2005 TCF Bank stepped forward with a commitment of $35 million that included naming rights. A bill to secure state funding failed in the final stages of the 2005 legislative session, but it had garnered substantial legislative support and received final approval the next year.

The new facility, costing $288.5 million, was built on a

parking lot across the street from Mariucci Arena and just a block from old Memorial Stadium. The public, which had never in the past responded to appeals for University athletic facilities, came up with $86 million in private funding including the final $6 million from Sanford, which allowed for the completion of a University of Minnesota sports Hall of Fame inside the new stadium.

In 2009, some 27 years after Gopher football had fled to downtown Minneapolis, the team returned to TCF Bank Stadium.

Full Circle

For the better part of the 20th century, there were two voices that defined Gopher football. For fans inside Memorial Stadium it was public address announcer Jules Perlt. For fans who got their Gopher football over the radio it was Ray Christensen.

Ray retired after the 2001 season after a 50-year career calling Gopher games. He felt it was time to step down, but he did so at the top of his game.

When it became clear that Gopher football was coming back to campus, it became equally clear that Ray should play some significant part in that return.

The question was posed to Ray and his wife, Ramona, at an event several months before the start of the 2009 season opener at TCF Bank Stadium.

Would Ray consider coming into the broadcast booth one more time at the start of the second half?

"I'd have to think about that," said the ever-modest Ray.

"He'll do it," said Ramona.

So plans were made for Ray to be in the booth from the start of the game against the Air Force Academy.

He arrived more than an hour before kickoff, not sure if anybody would know or care.

How wrong can one man be?

While Ray looked for time to finish his research and go

over his notes, camera crews impatiently waited to do interviews. As several of the interviews were shown briefly on the scoreboard, the fans applauded loudly at each glance of the legendary broadcaster.

During the first half Ray did what he always did, charting each and every offensive play in the same notebook he had used for many years.

As the end of the first half neared the cameras returned. This time they weren't so polite. They nudged one another to get the perfect angle. One of them, unbeknownst to Ray, was linked directly to the scoreboard.

As Dave Lee began to hand the play by play call off to Ray, several things happened. Not only did Ray's visage appear on the scoreboard, but also his voice was piped directly into the stadium public address system. While listeners to WCCO began to hear a familiar voice, viewers on the Big Ten network also got to listen to Ray.

Fans, almost as one, rose to face the broadcast booth. Many of them waved. Ray didn't notice. He was back in his element and he had work to do.

"Weber at quarterback. Keeps it. Drops back. Throwing it. Complete to Decker at the almost 15 and then he is rammed back. Hard."

It was vintage Christensen. A pleasant baritone with an economy of words.

Gopher football was back on campus and Ray was behind the mic.

Good times were back.